A Manager's Guide to Making Changes

A Manager's Guide to Making Changes

Arnold S. Judson

Management Consultant

1966

John Wiley & Sons Ltd.

London New York Sydney

First published 1966 by John Wiley & Sons Ltd.

Library of Congress catalog card number 65–28641

Printed and bound in Great Britain by
Hazell Watson & Viney Ltd
Aylesbury, Bucks

To June

Preface

In 1789 Ben Franklin wrote to a friend, 'But in this world nothing is certain but death and taxes'. He neglected to mention a third certainty . . . change. Changes have been, are, and will continue to be a continuous feature of our lives. The process of life itself involves a constant series of changes. Constancy has no part in life.

Business organizations, too, experience changes. Any organization operates within an economic environment that is continually changing. Changes in its external environment require that appropriate changes be made within the organization. It is necessary that its objectives, policies, organization structures, personnel and methods of operation be changed so that it can become or remain financially sound. Thus, we might say that each organization has needs requiring fulfilment, needs for changes aimed at maintaining economic viability and vitality.

Each of us who works in organizations also has needs requiring fulfilment. Although these needs are often manifold and complex, our need for maintaining our sense of security is usually paramount. The satisfaction of this need requires that our environment remain familiar and consistent; in short, unchanging.

There is, however, a fundamental conflict between the organization's need for change and our need for maintaining a sense of security. This conflict is thrown into sharp relief whenever changes are introduced within the organization. It is up to the management to find ways of resolving such conflict so that the organization's objectives are met. Their effectiveness in doing so has a direct bearing on how well the organization manages to improve or even to maintain its competitive or financial position in its economic environment.

The pressure for changes may originate both from within and from outside the organization. The management themselves may generate innovations, or they may be compelled to take action because of economic and political forces entirely external to the organization. Whether management are implementing their own desires for improvement, or whether they are reacting to external pressures, the manner in which they act to change the *status quo* will determine the long-term ability of the enterprise to survive.

How much any management achieve of the full benefits that could be derived from a change is determined by three independent variables:

* Their skill in identifying and analysing the objectives of that change, and those problems requiring solutions.

* Their skill in devising successful methods to accomplish these objectives and solve these problems.

* Their skill in gaining acceptance and support for both the objectives and the methods for their achievement from the people affected by and involved in the change.

Management must be skilful in all three of these respects in order to introduce and implement changes smoothly, and also to realize the maximum results possible. If management are deficient in any one of these respects, the potential benefits that could otherwise have resulted from a change would be reduced. Management's analysis of a problem might be brilliant. Their identification of the objectives that should be achieved might be correct. Their approach to the attainment of these objectives might be imaginative and clever. Yet, the expected results could not be realized if the managers were not also skilful in coping with any resistance to the change from those involved.

But can we expect managers to be skilful in all three of the above respects? Any manager, in relative isolation, can identify and analyse both the objectives and problems, and devise methods for their achievement and solution. To do these things well, he would require a keen, logical and imaginative mind, together with sufficient reliable data. When a manager performs these tasks, the outcome depends primarily on the extent of his own abilities.

However, a manager, no matter how brilliant, cannot alone achieve acceptance of and support for a change from those affected or otherwise involved. To do so, he must depend on others. Here, the manager is not in sole control of the situation. He alone cannot determine the outcome. He must be able to influence the thoughts and attitudes of those involved in the change to secure their co-operation. If he cannot do this, the change, no matter how well it was conceived, will to some extent fail.

Can managers improve their skills in introducing and implementing changes? A manager's ability to identify and analyse problems depends on his intellectual power. He can develop his skill in several ways: formal academic training; personal experience of trial and error; informed and constructive criticism from his seniors, peers or subordinates; and knowledge of the effects of his decisions. It is doubtful that he can do much to improve this skill through reading books only.

In the training of management, considerable attention has already been devoted to developing those skills involved in the invention of solutions to problems. One approach stemmed from the Gilbreths' techniques of work study and work simplification. 'Brainstorming' is a more recent attempt to free the mind and stimulate creative thinking.

However, comparatively few efforts have been made to develop methods for getting people to be more cooperative with respect to the changes in which they are directly involved. Yet, the solution to these problems can be found in a planned and systematic manner. A manager can develop some facility in coping with resistance and in gaining people's acceptance of changes.

In this book I have attempted to develop some concepts and principles to help managers improve the way in which they introduce and implement changes in business situations. Any capable manager should be able to apply these concepts.

The question of whether or not a change should be made, and how such a decision should be reached, is outside the scope of this book. To discuss this subject would require a treatment of the process of decision-making. In this book, I have assumed that the decision to make a change has already been reached. I have also assumed that the objectives of the change are in the best long-term interests of the organization. Our concern, then, is how can the change be made so that its full benefits are realized.

The ideas presented here are not intended to help managers manipulate their employees into accepting changes that are neither in their nor in the organization's best long-term interests. On the contrary, it is my hope that by applying these concepts management can become aware of any poorly conceived or miscalculated decisions in time to retract or alter them. At any rate, it is unlikely that any management could, by using the approaches suggested here, get their employees to accept a change that would ultimately prove harmful to them.

In the past decade, there has been an increasing amount of research done in the field of organization theory and its relevance to human behaviour. Still in its formative stages, this work will eventually constitute a significant contribution to management's knowledge and understanding of the dynamics of making changes in an organizational setting. Although this research has to date been far from conclusive, its findings have been suggestive. I have tried to incorporate some of the ideas emanating from this research into this book.

I should like to emphasize that the particular approaches discussed in the following pages should be regarded neither as proven principles nor as formulae that can be applied with certain success in any business situation. Further research will undoubtedly make it necessary to modify some of these concepts. Also, each change as well as each organization has its own unique characteristics. Often, these result in special problems. To solve these, managers will need to adapt and modify the approaches described here. Nevertheless, it is my hope that the fundamental principles underlying these approaches will prove to be broadly applicable in helping management improve their present ability to make changes.

I should like to express my grateful appreciation to Mr. Ronald Jacobs and Dr. Paul Watson for their helpful comments and suggestions in the preparation of this book.

ARNOLD S. JUDSON
London, February 1965

Contents

I Defining Change and its Causes

There is nothing in this world constant, but inconstancy.

JONATHAN SWIFT

* The desks in an office are rearranged to accommodate three new clerks and their equipment.

* An improvement is made in the quality of the rubber thread used in manufacturing golf balls. As a consequence, there is a reduction in the number of breaks occurring in this thread during the winding operation.

* As a result of studies made by industrial engineers, a machine operative is told that he will no longer be operating one paper-coating machine as had been his custom. Instead, in three days hence, he will be required to operate two coating machines simultaneously.

* A plant maintenance superintendent is told that in one week hence, instead of reporting to the plant manager, he will be reporting to a new manager of plant services, who will in turn be reporting to the plant manager.

* An announcement is made to the employees of the Ion Electronics Company, Ltd. that within the next six months the manufacturing facilities of this firm will be moving to a new plant. This will be located in Stevenage New Town, twenty miles away from their present location in London.

* The Board of Directors of Halox Photographic Products, Inc. decide to diversify their principal business of manufacturing and marketing cameras and film for amateur and professional use. They aim to enter the field of office duplicating equipment. Immediately, they begin planning for the design, development, manufacture and sale of these new products.

What are the common threads that link these six examples? How can these cases help us to clarify our definition of change in a business environment? And, how can these illustrations illuminate the basic reasons for changes?

Clearly, in all six cases, some aspect of the *status quo* either is about to change or is in the process of changing.

All six changes were instituted by management. They acted in each instance because of a need to change the existing situation. In some cases, this need was initiated by the manager. He desired to improve the efficiency of his operations, and saw a method for doing so. In other cases, the decision to act was a response to external pressures. These might have been initiated by more senior management, or by economic and political forces in the business environment. Whatever the primary source of the pressure to change, management decided to act because they hoped for certain improvements or benefits.

Some of these benefits will be immediate. Others will result in time. In several of the cases, only a segment of the company's operations is affected. In others, the entire organization will be involved. In these six examples, the scope of each change falls within a wide range. Nevertheless, we shall be able to develop some principles that can be used both to explain what is happening in these changes and to improve the way in which they are brought about.

In all six cases, others in addition to management are vitally involved. Some of these people will be affected directly by the changing circumstances. They will have to alter their established patterns of behaviour. Others will be required to contribute their efforts towards realizing the changes, but will not be affected directly. In every case, how many benefits or improvements result from each change depends on the behaviour both of those affected and of the managers and supervisors. In the next four chapters, we shall discuss the manner in which people are affected by change and the nature of their reactions.

Means or Ends?

If a manager is to carry out a change successfully, he must first understand fully what is about to happen. He must be able to answer the following questions:

* What is to be accomplished, and why?

* How is this to be accomplished?

* What will be changed as a consequence?

Only when a manager understands the answers to these questions about a particular change can he properly distinguish the means from the ends.

Why is such a distinction vital to the successful introduction and implementation of any change?

In most situations, it is the ends or objectives that are of paramount importance. Objectives can be defined both in immediate and in long-range terms. Because these might be quite different from one another, both types must be noted. Provided that the means used to achieve the objectives are ethical and moral, it matters little which are employed. What does matter is how well the desired long-range objectives can be accomplished by the particular means under consideration.

A manager must remain as flexible as possible in his ability to select or modify the means for achieving the desired objectives. His approach to a change can remain flexible if he can maintain a clear separation in his mind between the objectives and the methods for their accomplishment. When such a distinction is blurred, it is easy for the manager to confuse the methods with the objectives. The methods can themselves become the primary objectives. When this occurs, the manager can become so committed to one particular method that he loses both flexibility and objectivity.

But flexibility and objectivity are both essential to the success of a change. They are important at the outset. They continue to be important throughout the change until the objectives are achieved. Although one method might be appropriate at the start, it might become necessary to modify this method as the change progresses because of unpredictable developments in the situation. Also, modification of the method might become desirable as a result of worthwhile suggestions contributed by others involved. These suggestions may be offered at any time during the change. Because their adoption might increase the benefits from the change, the manager must maintain sufficient flexibility to incorporate these ideas in his introduction and implementation. To do so is both in his best interests and in those of the organization as well.

If a manager is himself resistant to changes while he is bringing one about, there is a reduced probability that he will achieve successful results. It would be difficult for such a manager to react appropriately to unexpected developments in the situation. It would also be difficult for him to make the best use of constructive criticism and suggestions. On the other hand, a manager who understands from the outset the differences between what is to be accomplished and how it is to be achieved will tend to be less resistant to subsequent alterations in the way he approaches the change. Consequently, he would be more likely to achieve successful results.

If we analyse the six case examples, we should be able to distinguish clearly methods from objectives. This analysis should also help us to see how the choice of objective can influence the method employed.

* *Rearranging the desks* was the method chosen to accomplish an immediate objective: providing for sufficient space to accommodate three new clerks, together with their desks, chairs and files. Although the longer-range goal was unspecified, it might have been to expand office activities so that an increase in business could be handled. In this case, the long-term objective is quite different from the immediate goal. If the immediate goal were regarded as the primary objective, then the rearrangement of the desks was an inevitable method for its accomplishment. If, however, the long-range goal was the objective, the following alternative methods might have been considered: (a) introducing more automation into the office without increasing the number of clerks; (b) simplifying clerical procedures without increasing the number of clerks; or (c) acquiring more space for expanding the office. Thus, although methods (a) and (b) might have been more desirable in the long run, they would not have been considered if only the immediate goal were taken as the objective to be accomplished.

* *Improving the quality of rubber thread* was the method chosen to accomplish the immediate objective of reducing the number

of thread breaks occurring during the winding of the golf balls. The long-range objectives were to reduce the manufacturing cost and to improve the quality of the product. In this case, both the immediate and long-term objectives are consistent. Nevertheless, alternative methods might have been considered: (a) redesigning the winding equipment; or (b) redesigning the method for maintaining a constant thread tension during the winding operation.

* *Doubling the number of coating machines to be operated by one man* was the method chosen to accomplish the immediate objective of improving the utilization of the operative's time. The long-term objective was to reduce operating costs so as to maintain or improve the profit margin. The immediate and long-term objectives are different but consistent. Yet there are alternative methods of approach, such as incorporating other functions (e.g. inspection, maintenance and record-keeping activities) into the operative's job. This approach could lead to a reduction in the number of service personnel required.

* *Changing the level of reporting of the plant maintenance superintendent* was the method chosen to accomplish the immediate objective of reducing the number of managers that reported directly to the plant manager. His longer-range objective might have been to free himself from some details of day-to-day operation so that he could devote more time to long-range planning and to the consideration of broader problems. These two objectives are different. If the plant manager had identified the longer-range goal as his objective, he might have considered as an alternative approach delegating more authority to his existing staff.

* *Moving manufacturing operations to a new plant* located in a nearby suburban area was the method chosen to accomplish two immediate goals: (a) modernizing the manufacturing process; and (b) providing for a possible future need to expand the business. These goals are consistent with the longer-term objectives of improving both the company's share of the market and the profitability of the business. Because all these objectives are broad, there is wide scope for alternative methods for their accomplishment. Other locations closer to the present plant might have been selected for the new factory. The existing plant

might have been rebuilt and modernized. Or it might have been closed altogether, and manufacturing operations could have been either subcontracted or reinstituted in an entirely new area.

* *To diversify products* was the method selected to accomplish the long-term objectives of: (a) improving the company's financial position; (b) ensuring the firm's financial stability; and (c) reducing seasonal fluctuations in both sales and operating activities. As in the previous case there are many alternative methods that might have been employed to accomplish these objectives.

The Nature of Change and Its Causes

We can now reach some conclusions about the nature of change and its causes.

Change can be defined for our purposes in this book as any alteration that is initiated by management in an individual's work situation or work environment.

It is essential to identify the objectives for which any particular change is a method of accomplishment. The necessity for and value of these objectives must be questioned and justified before they are accepted. Immediate goals must be distinguished from long-term objectives. Any inconsistencies that exist between short- and long-term objectives must be recognized. Generally, when objectives are long-term, they permit considerable variety in the choice of methods for their accomplishment. If he is to maximize his chances for success, a manager must have the widest possible choice in the method of change. Therefore, he should avoid any restrictions that may be inherent in a concern with immediate goals, and define his objectives in long-range terms.

There are about six types of long-term objectives mostly likely to create the need for changes within business organizations:

* *Improving the product* in terms of quality, uniformity, visual design, functional design, extension of function.

* *Improving sales* volume and services.

* *Improving profitability* as a consequence of increased operating effectiveness, lower operating costs, better utilization of personnel, equipment, materials and money.

* *Improving the company's public image* in terms of better relations with customers, suppliers and the general public.

* *Improving human relationships within the organization* in terms of better teamwork, less friction and less diversion of human energies towards activities that are non-productive, and better opportunities for the employees to realize to the full their potential capabilities.

* *Improving the ability of the organization to cope with anticipated future conditions and problems* such as changes in the market for the products, changes in the technology of equipment, materials and methods, and changes in the size and nature of the organization itself.

It might be useful to list the more common types of changes that could be employed to accomplish these objectives:

Changes in the methods of operation

Ways in which work is performed
Location of work
Layouts of work areas
Nature of materials used
Nature of plant and facilities
Machinery, tools and equipment
Safety and housekeeping practices
Operating procedures

Changes in products

Specifications of products
Specifications of the manufacturing (or other) process
Component materials
Standards of quality

Changes in organization

Structure of organization and allocation of responsibilities
Levels of supervision
Extent of delegation
Size and nature of work groups
Supervision of work groups
Placement of individuals in jobs

Changes in the working environment

Working conditions
Systems of reward and punishment
Standards of performance
Policies and procedures

Summary

When a manager is about to introduce and implement a change, before he takes any action at all he should first answer several questions for himself:

* *What is to be accomplished and why?*

* *Why is it necessary to make any change at all, and what will be the value of doing so?*

* *What are the methods to be used for accomplishing the long-range objectives?*

* *What precisely will be changed as a consequence of the particular method selected?*

Clarifying these points at the outset should help the manager to have the widest possible choice of methods in his accomplishment of the objectives. Also, it should be easier for him to be more flexible in the way he manages the changing situation because he would be able, whenever necessary, to modify his original approach and to incorporate any worthwhile ideas contributed by others. Consequently, there will be a greater probability that the change will be implemented successfully.

2

How People Are Affected by Changes

All changes are irksome to the human mind, especially those which are attended with great dangers and uncertain effects.

JOHN ADAMS

IN THE preceding chapter, we noted that every change has some impact on people. They are the operatives, clerks and other workers who must alter their behaviour so that the objectives of the change can be achieved. They are the other workers who might later be affected by the outcome. They are also the foremen and other supervisors at the lower levels of the management hierarchy. They are the managers responsible for carrying out the change. They are the staff specialists who are invited to contribute their expert knowledge. And they are the union stewards and officials who represent the workers involved. Those affected most are all those directly involved in carrying out management's intentions. But all these people must alter both their attitudes and behaviour to some extent before the full benefits of the change can be realized.

A manager can achieve the maximum benefits from a change only if he is able to minimize any resistance to it by those affected. In order to minimize resistance and maximize acceptance, he must first understand the nature of resistant behaviour, of resistant attitudes and feelings, and of the complex, dynamic relationship that exists between these and the several factors that influence them. These factors derive from three sources: the individuals affected by the change; its organizational setting, its culture, environment and context; and the nature of the change itself.

In the following three chapters, we shall examine those factors that influence both attitudes and behaviour, and that derive from all three of these sources. We shall then discuss the relationship between resistant attitudes and resistant behaviour. Finally, we shall develop a method by which management might anticipate in their planning how those affected might react to an intended change.

Before we can analyse attitudes and behaviour, however, we must first consider the objective effects that changes have on the people involved. We must understand the nature of the impact of a change on those affected, so that we can establish a frame of reference for our consideration of resistant attitudes and behaviour. In this chapter, then, we shall examine three distinct ways in which people are affected by changes. One of these is whatever alterations in behaviour are made necessary. Another effect is whatever changes occur to the way in which each individual relates to and regards his work. The remaining effect is whatever alterations are made to established relationships among those affected and between them and the organization.

Behavioural Effects

The most evident effect of any change is the objective alterations that must be made by those doing the work to the physical routines by which the work is performed. The following instances should serve to illustrate some typical behavioural effects of changes on people:

* Mary is told that several of her movements in assembling electronic amplifiers are no longer necessary if she rearranges the sequence of the assembly operations. Mary must therefore adjust herself to a different sequence of operations as well as to different arm–hand–finger movements.

* A new automatic machine is introduced to replace the skilled manual process of sewing buttonholes in men's clothing. Those skilled workers who had been sewing buttonholes must now either become machine operatives or learn entirely different skills.

* The intensity of illumination is increased in an office. The clerks must adjust themselves to the new lighting conditions.

* The stockroom in a machine shop is moved from its centralized location to one corner of the shop. Some of the craftsmen will

have to walk further than before to get their tools, while others will walk less.

* There is a reduction of 12% in the tensile strength of paper that is receiving several chemical coatings. The operatives of the coating machines must either adjust themselves to a greater frequency of breaks in the paper, or they must learn new techniques of handling it.

* All the employees in a company are notified that they must wear safety glasses at all times while they are in particular sections of the laboratories. These employees must learn to don their safety glasses whenever they enter these areas.

Thus, the behavioural effects of a change cause people to alter the way in which they perform their work.

Such alterations in behaviour are, in fact, the immediate point of the change. Its successful implementation usually depends on such alterations. But these alterations in behaviour do not simply occur automatically at management's request or direction. The precise alterations desired will come about only with the active cooperation of those directly involved, and the extent and nature of their cooperation will depend in part on their attitudes. The formation of these attitudes is profoundly influenced by the psychological and social effects of the change.

Psychological Effects

Another kind of impact that changes have on people can be termed the psychological effects. Any change will tend to alter the way in which each individual relates to and feels about what he is doing. When a change is first announced, everyone affected begins to wonder what the change will mean to him with respect to his future manner of working. He will have a number of questions about this, because at first any change creates uncertainty. Often, such uncertainty is related to the individual's ability to cope with the changes in his work pattern. As we shall discuss in the following chapter, both the variety of one's questions and the intensity of one's feelings depend primarily on one's personality and experiences. However, the *likelihood* that certain types of questions will be stimulated is a consequence of objective elements of the change itself. Thus, the likelihood that certain questions will arise is predictable. Let us consider two examples:

* A new and extremely complicated automatic machine is introduced to perform several operations together. These were previously done on several more simple machines. Brian, an operative on the old equipment, is selected to run the new machine. This change would be likely to stimulate several questions in Brian's mind. These questions would tend to arise whatever the nature of his personality and experience. He would probably wonder, for example, how well he will be able to master the new technology and skills required, and how well he will meet the new standards of the job. Also, it is likely that he would wonder whether or not he will be compensated fairly for what he considers will be his new, added responsibilities.

* Stephen is the manager of a branch office located in a provincial city. He is promoted to a position in the company's head office in London. He has never before lived there. Without any knowledge of Stephen's personality or background, we can predict that this change would tend to raise several questions in his mind. He would probably wonder how well he will adjust to an environment where the pressures on him will be perhaps greater, and certainly different. He would also wonder about the effects of this move on his future financial position.

Thus, because of the psychological effects of a change, we can predict that certain questions are likely to occur to each individual affected. These questions will concern his relationship to the changed manner in which he will be working.

Social Effects

Changes also generate social effects. These effects are the alterations that take place in the individual's established relationships with the others in his work group and with his management, union and the organization as a whole.

Almost any change in the pattern or method of work will tend to alter the relationships that have become established among those doing the job and between them and other workers or colleagues in the organization, their supervisors and their subordinates. Often, the basic framework for these relationships (the need for interactions and their frequency) is established by the technology and organization of the work, together with its physical environment. For example, the pattern of interactions among a group working on an assembly-line is different from that of teams of individuals all performing the identical operation. Other aspects of the working environment that affect the pattern of interactions are the physical location of the operations, the level of skills involved, the means by which the work is progressed from one point to another and the pay system.

In addition to the basic framework for relationships set by the technology and organization of the work and its environment, the nature of these relationships is determined in large part by the individual personal needs of the people involved. All of us tend to adjust the nature of our social relationships to fit certain needs arising out of our individual personalities. It is likely that anyone who has worked on a particular job for an appreciable length of time will have tried to satisfy some of his personal needs by establishing rapport with others in his working environment. When the procedures and systems of work are changed, these comfortable and satisfying relationships are often disrupted or altered.

As with the psychological effects, the social effects of a change cause those involved to wonder what alterations will be taking place in their existing relationships. They will also wonder about the nature of their future relationships. Here too, if we know enough about these existing relationships and about the intended change we can then predict the likelihood that certain questions will arise.

Let us reconsider the prior two cases of Brian and Stephen in the light of the social effects involved:

* Brian, in his new job as a machine operative, will be relatively isolated in a new location. He will be separated from his present workmates. Although we know nothing about Brian as an individual, it is likely that such a change would raise certain questions in his mind. He would tend to wonder how he will feel about being cut off from the opportunities of chatting with his fellow workers. Also, he would probably be concerned that in the future he will be less well informed about what is going on around him in the organization. He would also be likely to wonder how his performance on the new job will affect how his supervisor, his workmates and his union will now regard him. Finally, he might also wonder about the effects of this change on his general future in the organization.

* As a consequence of his impending move from the provinces to London, Stephen, the promoted branch manager, would un-

doubtedly have some questions about his new social situation. He would probably wonder how well he will be able to cope with many other competing managers in an environment where political considerations are often paramount. This environment will be very different from his familiar one. There, he was the most senior executive. He would probably wonder about his feelings at the loss of status as an important member of the provincial community. Also, he would be likely to have questions about what kind of a person he will now be working for. Another likely concern would be the effect of this move on his future career with the company.

A third example might help us to clarify further the nature of these social effects:

* A group of widely separated, noisy machines are used to wind rubber thread on to cores for the manufacture of golf balls. The operatives depend on Arthur, their supplier of materials, for communicating with each other and for maintaining contact with what is going on around them in the organization. Because the rubber thread broke frequently, fresh spools were often required. Also, the spools of defective thread had to be removed. Arthur performed both these tasks, and his contacts with each operative were frequent. When a different company was contracted to supply thread, its quality improved greatly and the number of breaks diminished sharply. As a consequence, Arthur had fewer contacts with the operatives. Thus the entire social situation was altered. As a result, instead of receiving a wholehearted welcome from the operatives, the improvement in quality was regarded with mixed feelings.

The social effects of a change can have critical consequences on the way in which it is regarded, particularly when there is a possibility of alterations in personal status. Such is the case in any organizational change, whether it be in terms of structure or of personnel.

Importance of the Psychological and Social Effects

In the past sixty years, considerable attention and effort have been devoted to improving methods for dealing with the behavioural effects of changes. Many techniques have been developed and applied to make it easier for people to alter their routines for performing work: engineering design, time and motion study, work simplification, industrial engineering and industrial training techniques.

However, although increasing attention and effort have been devoted in recent industrial research to developing ways of dealing with the psychological and social effects of changes, the results of this work have yet to be widely applied in business. Certainly, the level of sophistication achieved in this area is in no way as high as it is in engineering, industrial engineering and the training of skills.

Yet, if a change is to be introduced and implemented successfully, *all three* effects must be considered and dealt with positvely. Often, the success of a change depends primarily on how it is perceived by everyone involved. Without acceptance and support, even changes that are brilliantly conceived and that are obvious improvements are likely to yield disappointing results. The following examples should illustrate this point:

* The engineering department of a company manufacturing hypodermic syringes developed a high-speed automatic machine that was capable of increasing the rate of manufacture of the syringe body. This production rate could be increased from 400 to 1500 bodies per hour. There was a history of mistrust and hostility between the management and labour of this firm. When the new machine was unveiled, the union representatives stated that they did not believe the machine could increase the production rate to more than 700 bodies per hour. Because this figure was less than half the amount predicted by the engineers, the management protested vigorously. Nevertheless, after the machine was installed, the production rate gradually rose to about 700 and then levelled off.

* In Great Britain, the heavy tank trucks used to deliver petroleum products were limited by law to a maximum speed of 20 m.p.h. As a consequence of modified legislation, this maximum speed was subsequently raised to 30 m.p.h. The industry-wide agreement between the Transport and General Workers Union and the association of petroleum companies was amended to provide a bonus payment of sixpence per hour 'for achieving the full improvement in running times from 30 m.p.h. operation'. Most drivers were infuriated with what they regarded as a paltry pay settlement. As a consequence, the average driving

speeds at many operating points were actually reduced rather than increased.

Summary

Any change has three kinds of effects on the people involved. The behavioural effects are whatever alterations they must make to the way in which they do their work. The psychological effects are whatever alterations are made to the way in which individuals relate to and regard their work. The social effects are the changes that occur to the established relationships among those involved and between them and the organization. Both the psychological and social effects tend to stimulate questions in the minds of the people involved. When enough is known about the nature of both the existing situation and the intended change, it is possible to predict that certain kinds of questions will probably arise.

For a change to be realized successfully, management must act positively in dealing with all its effects: behavioural, psychological and social. Before such action can be taken, however, managers must understand as much as possible about the way these effects cause the people affected to have particular attitudes towards the change. In the following chapter, we shall discuss the relationship between these effects and attitudes.

3 Factors that Influence an Individual's Attitudes Towards a Change

No passion so effectually robs the mind of all its powers of acting and reasoning as fear.

EDMUND BURKE

Change is not only an intellectual process but a psychological one as well.

PETER DRUCKER

WE HAVE already described how the psychological and social effects of a change tend to stimulate certain predictable kinds of questions in the minds of those involved. Each person will then find that many of these questions will evoke feelings and attitudes. These derive both from his own individual personality and background of experience, and from a variety of factors in the situation. These questions, feelings and attitudes can have a profound effect on the way that each individual regards the change. Furthermore, how he actually behaves when he becomes involved in the change will be determined by the interaction of these attitudes with other forces generated by the group and by the organization as a whole.

If management are to achieve maximum benefits from any change, they must create and maintain an atmosphere that will serve to minimize resistant behaviour and encourage acceptance and support. Also, they must be able to anticipate many of the specific questions and problems that are likely to arise as a consequence of the change. Management can create the proper atmosphere and cope with these problems only if they understand the dynamics of the relationship between attitudes and behaviour, both with individuals and groups.

We should like to emphasize at this point that the relationship between attitudes and behaviour is not a direct one. That is, someone who feels apprehensive and resistant towards a change may not necessarily resist it in a manner that directly reflects his attitude. Rather, he might behave in a way that apparently may be quite unrelated to his actual feelings. But his feelings may nevertheless influence his behaviour in other, more subtle, ways. We shall discuss this in the next two chapters.

Let us consider, first, the factors that influence attitudes. Although we can predict that a particular change is likely to stimulate certain questions in the minds of the group affected, is it possible to predict how each member will regard that change? What will be his specific questions? What feelings and attitudes will be evoked by these questions? What will he fear? What will he hopefully expect? How intense will be his feelings and attitudes? Finally, what will be the relationship between these feeings and attitudes and the way he actually behaves?

Clearly, our understanding of human motivation and of organizational theory has not yet reached the level of sophistication where we can make accurate predictions with certainty. It is possible, however, to accumulate sufficient information about the nature of any particular change, about the particular individuals involved and about the organizational environment and context in which they are operating, so that many of their probable reactions can be forecast and anticipated. Such estimates cannot be entirely accurate. Nor can they be all-inclusive. Nevertheless, despite their limitations, these forecasts can be extremely useful in planning for the introduction and implementation of that change. This and the next two chapters are concerned with how such estimates can be developed.

When any of us are confronted with a change that is to affect us, our attitude towards it is influenced by several complex factors. Some are functions primarily of our own individual personality. Others arise primarily from more objective elements in the organizational environment and its context. The remaining factors stem from the conflicts that are generated by the change and its manner of institution between our own interests and those of the organization. All these factors interact in a complicated way to determine our individual feelings and attitudes.

Predisposed Feeling About any Change

One of the factors that influences our attitudes towards a change is both individual and deeply personal. It is a rather vague, predisposed feeling about changes of any kind. This feeling is likely to be deeply ingrained in our mind. It is unlikely even that we are aware of its existence. We would certainly be unable to describe it. Yet it often influences our attitude towards any specific change.

What is the source of this deeply ingrained feeling? To understand this, we must remember how we developed towards maturity. From the moment we were born, all of us were faced with a continuing series of changes, the earlier ones being especially profound. In birth, the relatively cold and hostile world outside was substituted for the warm comfort of the womb. Such a change must have evoked unpleasant and distasteful feelings. Next, many of us experienced another profound change, that of being weaned from mother's nipple to that of a bottle. Again, this substitution of an impersonal object for one that was warm, reassuring and comfortable must have been unpleasant.

Further profound changes occurred during our early years. Learning to deposit body wastes in toilets required us for the first time to exercise control over our bodily functions. This was far less pleasant than the freedom we previously enjoyed. Then, if we were the first child in the family, the sudden appearance of an infant brother or sister must have been unsettling, because we then had to share the previously exclusive attention of our parents. Later, our initial introduction to school may well have generated mixed feelings of both anxiety and pleasure.

These profound changes are experiences that all of us have in common. Furthermore, these changes were, in most instances, imposed on us without the benefit of discussion or consultation, and therefore without our understanding. In no case could we really have understood what was happening to us, or why. All of these changes involved our giving up pleasures that yielded almost instantaneous gratifications. Although other pleasures were substituted in their place (e.g. parental approval and affection), the gratifications from these new pleasures were not necessarily as immediately satisfying. We had to learn to accept the increased time lag between our action and the pleasure and gratification that followed.

It is very difficult for a young child to forgo immediate gratifications for others that might come later on. For example, it is unlikely that an infant could be persuaded to give up a lolly that he is sucking for a promised bag of lollies, thirty minutes later. The natural reaction of any child to such changes (particularly the significant changes of his childhood) is to resist them. Initially, at least, these changes are unpleasant. It should not be surprising, therefore, that we tend to develop in our earliest years some suspicion and distrust of changes. The memories of unpleasant experiences with these significant childhood changes, and of the feelings of suspicion and distrust that were associated with them, tend to be persistent during adulthood.

Although everyone has undergone these early experiences, the resultant effect on any adult's fundamental attitude towards changes varies widely. The cause of this variation stems both from the manner in which these early changes were handled by parents and from the nature of the individual's inherited strengths and weaknesses.

There is an enormous difference between the demands made on a child by parents who are patient, flexible and understanding and those made by parents who are rigid and unreasonable. Parents with the former characteristics can help their child to realize that there can be certain compensations for the loss of pleasures that yield immediate gratifications. If the rewards offered for making the change are sufficiently great (e.g. approval and love), then the child may regard the making of future changes in a more attractive light. Any element of unpleasantness in such a child's experience of these changes might have been greatly minimized. As an adult, he might not regard changes with suspicion and distrust. He might be able to face an unknown future with some self-confidence. If he were to have questions about a change, they would tend to be objective and based on the realities of the situation, instead of on vague apprehensions and fears.

On the other hand, the child whose parents were unyielding and constantly making unreasonable demands to which he was forced to conform might have developed very different fundamental feelings about changes. To such a child, every major change was probably an agonizing experience. As an adult, he would tend to regard almost every change with suspicion and fear. He would probably be reluctant to submit himself to an unknown future, the inevitable consequence of any change. It is likely that he would conjure up a wide variety of questions about how the change might affect him. These questions would probably be based more on his personal fears and imaginings than on the realities of what is about to take place.

Why can we draw this parallel between the changes experienced as adults and those experienced as children? All changes involve giving up the familiar for the unfamiliar, the certain for the uncertain. In any present situation, both the sources and nature of gratification are known. When one is confronted with a change, one is faced with a future situation in which both the sources of gratification and the gratifications themselves are either unknown or uncertain. No one in such circumstances can know with assurance what is really about to happen to him. Thus, his perception of the impending change and of what he imagines will happen to him become especially important in shaping his attitudes towards the change.

From an adult's childhood experiences with changes he retains a legacy in the form of a residue of faint but persistent memories. These memories from the past can exert a pervasive influence on his attitudes when he faces changes in the present. For many, the prospect of an unknown or uncertain future stimulates primarily doubts and fears. A measure of courage and self-assurance is required to enter into any new situation. It is a rare person who can undergo changes with comfort and confidence.

Feelings of Insecurity

Very closely related to our predisposed feelings about changes is another individual and deeply personal factor that influences our attitudes when we are confronted with a changing situation. This factor is the extent to which we feel generally secure. Such feelings are based primarily on our individual personalities. They are, however, to a limited extent also a reflection of the realities of our financial status. Clearly, anyone with independent means is less likely to fear changes affecting his job than the person depending entirely on his wages or salary for his income.

The extent to which we feel secure is primarily a result of our cumulative experiences since birth. As in the case of our predisposed feelings about change, we would find it difficult to express or recognize any feelings of insecurity. These, too, would be deeply ingrained and would have a profound influence on many aspects of our behaviour.

These feelings are particularly important because they can cause a person to have fears without objective justification. Such a person would tend to be apprehensive about any events that he might interpret as having a potentially adverse effect on him. He would probably find many more reasons for objecting to a particular change than would someone who felt more secure.

Futhermore, how secure or insecure we may feel has an effect on other aspects of our behaviour. These feelings are closely related to self-confidence. They are also related to the extent of our resourcefulness and initiative. Finally, they determine in part how flexible and adaptable we are.

Relevance of Feelings about Changes and Security

Of what value to managers is an understanding of these deeply-ingrained feelings about changes and security? Certainly, these feelings are beyond the reach of any manager's ability to influence them. We might even question whether or not they can be altered at all to any appreciable extent.

Nevertheless, it is important that managers appreciate the existence of these feelings. Managers must realize that most people have some suspicion and discomfort when facing any change. They must also recognize that it is their task to minimize these feelings (it is these same feelings that probably account for the glib reference to the 'fact' that 'it is human nature to resist change'). Furthermore, any manager who truly understands the nature of these feelings would realize that in any group of people who are about to be affected by a change each member will regard it somewhat differently from the others. Each individual will have his own special questions, fears and expectations. Also, these will vary from person to person both in their variety and intensity.

Therefore, any manager about to implement a change should not assume that everyone involved will regard it alike. Instead, he must expect that despite any apparent similarities in their behaviour their attitudes will be varied. These will range from opposition that is unreasoning and intense to some kind of acceptance, however uncomfortable and resigned it may be.

From his prior experiences and knowledge of his employees, a manager should be able to predict who will probably have feelings of opposition and who will tend to be more accepting. Sometimes, the manager should be able to predict whether or not these feelings of opposition are likely to be intense. Clearly, then, an intimate and detailed knowledge of each individual involved in the change is a necessary prerequisite for predicting individual behaviour. But, as we shall discuss later, such predictions may not be as fruitful as alternative approaches.

Cultural Beliefs and Norms

Those cultural beliefs and norms of behaviour that are characteristic of the societies in which we operate are also an influence on our attitudes towards changes. All of us operate simultaneously in several different societies, each with its own culture: the work group; the department or division of the organization; the organization as a whole; the community; the region; the nation; etc. Each of these societies has identifiable cultural beliefs and behavioural norms.

The existence and significance of cultural beliefs have been long familiar to anthropologists. In their study of primitive societies they were able to identify in each particular culture certain implicit ideas that were universally accepted and unquestioned. Typically, these ideas were concerned with the value of both objects and practices. Because of these ideas, certain practices were institutionalized as rituals, and became an essential element in the lives of the members of these primtive societies. Here is an example of a cultural belief held by such a primitive society:

> In the Betsileo and Tanala societies on the island of Madagascar, there existed the cultural belief that a child born on an 'unlucky' day would ultimately destroy its family. As a consequence of this belief, children born in a particular month were killed either by being drowned or by having cattle walk over them. Children born on other 'unlucky' days at other times of the year were thrown on the village rubbish heap for a period, or were washed in a jug of dirty dishwater. These practices were supposed to avert evil destiny.[1]

In our contemporary societies certain cultural beliefs also exist, although these may appear to have somewhat of a more rational basis than the one cited above.

Much of the recent research in the area of the relationship between personality and culture has led to the conclusion that man tends to create culture and society to fulfil his own needs.[2]

[1] A. Kardiner and R. Linton, *The Individual and His Society*, Columbia University Press, New York, 1939.

[2] For example, see:

C. Kluckholn and H. A. Murray, *Personality*, Knopf, New York, 1949.
T. M. Newcomb, *Social Psychology*, Dryden Press, New York, 1950.
K. Lewin, *Resolving Social Conflicts*, Harper, New York, 1949.
J. Gellin (ed.), *For a Science of Social Man*, Macmillan, New York, 1954.

The creation of a culture with its associated beliefs and behavioural norms provides us with a means for ensuring an outlet for the expression of our needs and tendencies towards particular forms of action.

Once established, any culture tends to exert an influence on the attitudes and behaviour of its members (especially the more recent entrants) to conform to the accepted beliefs and norms. After considerable time in a culture, this cultural and group pressure may cause a member to develop new needs. These are a rationalization of his more deeply-ingrained, fundamental needs which would otherwise be in conflict with the cultural (or organizational) conditions and demands.[1] It is for this reason that the question of relevance has been raised about a concern for the more fundamental personal needs in the study of behaviour in organizations, particularly during periods of change.

In any business organization (as well as in its subdivisions) there are cultural beliefs concerned with the value of or necessity for perpetuating certain practices. As in primitive societies, these beliefs are accepted implicitly. They are rarely, if ever, questioned.

Let us consider some examples of cultural beliefs and behavioural norms that exist both in British and in some American business organizations. Despite the general acceptability of the positive values that have been attached to these practices, each can in fact be challenged.

* Skilled workers must have 'mates' to assist them.

* Continued overtime in large amounts is an essential and unavoidable element of work schedules.

* Skilled workers must not perform any work that they consider to be outside the boundaries of their craft.

* Long service with a single organization is intrinsically desirable.

[1] The process by which differences in needs and goals of individuals and the organization and the subgroups of which they are members become rationalized has been termed by E. W. Bakke the fusion process (E. W. Bakke, *The Fusion Process*, Yale Labor & Management Center, New Haven, 1953). He theorizes that in this process all three elements (e.g. the individuals, the organization, the subgroup) are changed, and their behaviour maintains the integrity of the organization in the face of divergent interests which each holder hopes to realize through contact with the others.

* The length of an employee's service with an organization should be the determinant of his 'rights' to tenure, of the extent of his benefits and of his 'rights' to advancement.

* The extent of perquisites should be proportional to the status of the job.

In any change, the prevailing cultural beliefs and behavioural norms become an important factor when they influence people's attitudes towards it. This occurs when the real or imagined effects of the change are in direct conflict with the established cultural belief or norm. For example:

> A change is proposed that would result in the elimination of craftsmen's 'mates'. Both the craftsmen and the mates react immediately by dismissing this proposal as nonsense. They believe implicitly that the craftsmen–mate system is both useful and necessary. They cannot conceive that this system could possibly be eliminated.

Any manager, therefore, must be aware of both the existence and the potential significance of established cultural beliefs and norms. He should be able to identify those beliefs and norms that are prevalent in the cultures both of his organization and its subdivisions. With this knowledge, he can recognize when a specific change is in conflict with one or more of these cultural beliefs and norms. He should then be able to minimize such conflicts. Before it is possible to carry out a change that is in conflict with cultural beliefs, it is necessary first that the beliefs themselves be changed.

Trust

Another factor that influences an individual's attitudes towards a change stems from the nature of his relationships in the organization and its subgroups of which he is a member. The more important relationships are those with his immediate supervisor, with his manager, with his colleagues or fellow workers, with the organization as a whole and with his union. The key element in all these relationships is trust and loyalty.

If he has considerable trust in his supervisors and manager, he would probably have faith that whatever the change his welfare will be looked after. If, on the other hand, there is little trust, he would find it difficult to believe any promises. Thus anyone's willingness to change depends in part on how much he trusts his management.

Similarly, how much anyone trusts his union or his fellow workers to help protect his interests may also influence his attitudes towards a change. If he is confident that his interests will be protected, he might be more favourably inclined to 'go along with it', especially on an experimental basis. On the other hand, a lack of confidence in the power of either his union or his workmates might cause him to feel more opposed to the change. Such an attitude might stem from a belief that his future security depended primarily on his own ability to protect his interests.

Feelings of trust and loyalty between individuals are formed at first by the way in which the two personalities interact and 'hit it off'. But these feelings become established only after a series of incidents 'prove' that the supervisor, manager or fellow worker really is to be trusted. The opportunity to experience such incidents is affected by the frequency of relevant interactions which are permitted by the technology of the operation and the organizational circumstances. Established cultural beliefs also influence the development of feelings of trust. But only through direct observation and personal experience can one develop a deep conviction that one's trust is justified.

Loyalty and trust for the more abstract 'company', 'management' or 'union' are also developed through a series of direct personal experiences. However, because these are less frequent and often more impersonal and symbolic, the cultural beliefs may be more important in their influence. Certainly, it is unlikely that any individual either could or would have the desire to disprove for himself a prevailing cultural belief about the insincerity or general untrustworthiness of management.

There is also some evidence that a supervisor is trusted more when it is believed that he has a significant amount of influence with his superiors.[1]

> When supervisors who were found to have above-average influence or power with their own superior followed procedures considered generally to be good supervisory behaviour, their subordinates reacted favourably. On the other hand, when supervisors with below-average influence upwards practised the same desirable supervisory procedures, they failed to

[1] D. C. Pelz, 'Influence, a key to effective leadership for the first line supervisor', *Personnel*, No. 29, November 1952.

obtain a favourable reaction from their subordinates, and often the reaction was an adverse one. From these findings, Pelz termed upwards influence a 'conditioning variable', affecting the results of supervisory behaviour.

At the point when he is about to institute a change, a manager cannot alter the patterns of trust that have become established between himself and his employees and between them and the union and the organization as a whole. Such alterations can be achieved only over an extended period of time. Nevertheless, the manager must recognize both the significance and the nature of the patterns of trust that already exist. In effect, these are 'givens' in the situation at the time of the change.

The manager must accept that if there is little trust his problems of carrying out the change will be far more difficult than they would be if there were considerable trust. A little-trust situation can be counterbalanced somewhat by providing explicit and firm facts and guarantees, and by a gradual introduction of the change on the basis of a series of experimental trials. But when there is little trust the manager must recognize that his efforts to gain acceptance must be increased greatly. Even then, the likelihood of his achieving successful results will be considerably less than it might otherwise have been.

Historical Events

Our attitudes towards any change are also influenced by the objective historical events that have preceded it. The significant ones are those relevant to the change, and that occurred in the particular organization, in the local region, and possibly in the entire nation.

Those relevant historical events in the organization are:

* Its past policies, practices and customs.
* The nature of its past and present managements.
* The extent to which these managements have proved themselves trustworthy.
* The manner in which past changes have been carried out.
* The nature of the after-effects of these past changes.

The important historical factors of the region or nation are:

* The patterns of unemployment.
* The nature of opportunities for alternative employment.
* The forces that influence the mobility of labour.
* The extent of government involvement or control with respect to business.

These historical events can be important in the formation of attitudes towards changes. People often regard past events as precedents for what is likely to occur in the future. These events are often cited as 'evidence' of management's true attitudes towards achieving changes. Assumptions are often made that because events followed a particular course in the past this pattern will be repeated in the future.

As with the established patterns of trust, managers can do nothing about the existence of those historical events relevant to a particular change. These happenings cannot be undone. Nor can they be ignored. The manager must be aware of their existence. Furthermore, he should be able to identify those events of special relevance to the change at hand. With such knowledge, he should be able to act so as to counter-balance the influence of those historical events with a potentially negative effect on the formation of attitudes. Likewise, he might also be able to exploit advantageously those past happenings that might have a beneficial effect on attitudes towards the change.

Apprehensions and Expectations

Our attitudes towards a particular change are influenced by the specific apprehensions and hopeful expectations that are a direct consequence of any conflict or harmony between our personal needs and those of the organization. We have already noted that we have both fundamental needs that are a function of our personalities and more superficial needs that we adopt from the established beliefs and norms of the organizational cultures in which we operate.

Any organization has its own needs. Its most compelling need is to survive in a state of homeostatic equilibrium with its environment.[1] Most changes introduced by management are aimed at

[1] C. Argyris in 'Understanding human behaviour in organizations', *Modern Organization Theory* (ed. M. Haire), Wiley, New York, 1959, proposes as a

this end (see pp. 6–7). These changes, however, often bring into sharp focus conflicts between both the immediate and long-term needs of the organization and those of the people involved. Sometimes, these needs will be more in harmony than in conflict.

When changes are introduced, those involved become acutely aware of any conflicts or harmony between their interests and those of the organization. When there is harmony, the individual tends to feel reassured and expectant. When there is conflict, he may become apprehensive and fearful. Specific questions about his future may arise.

Because both each situation and the individuals involved are unique in their characteristics, we can describe the specific questions that might be stimulated in a particular person's mind by a particular change only in terms of probabilities and examples. The following questions should serve to illustrate the range of possibilities. Certainly, no single individual would have all these questions about any one change. Moreover, this list should not be considered as a complete compilation of all the questions that could occur for any change. Yet any manager about to carry out a change should be prepared to encounter and cope with questions such as these.

The individual in relation to the way in which the work is to be done

* How effective will I be in the new situation?

* What new things will I have to learn? Can I learn them? How difficult will it be for me? How much time will I have to learn these things?

* What are the new standards I shall have to meet? Will I be able to meet them?

* Will there be anything in the new situation that I shall find unpleasant or distasteful?

* Will the new situation involve increased responsibility for me? Will more work be required of me? Will I receive increased recognition?

---

definition of an organization that it is: (a) a plurality of parts; (b) each achieving specific objectives; and (c) maintaining themselves through their interrelatedness; and (d) simultaneously adapting to the external environment; therefore (e) maintaining the interrelated state of the parts.

* How will the new situation compare with my existing one in terms of job interest? Variety? Challenge? Satisfactions? Rewards?

* They are asking me to do something unprecedented. Can it be done?

The individual in relation to his work group

Fellow members of the work group

* How will the new situation affect my present contacts with my workmates? Will there be more or less contact? Will the people be the same, or will I have to work with a new group or with some new people?

* What will the change mean in terms of how others will regard me? What will they think? What will be my status in the eyes of others?

* Will I be able to continue my associations with my mates or colleagues as now? Will I be left out of things?

* How will the others feel about my cooperating with this change? Will they think I am being a 'company man'? Will I be setting any precedents that might hurt others later on? How will all this affect my future relationships?

* Will others lose their jobs as a consequence of this change?

* Will I continue to be as well informed about what is going on in the group (or organization) as I am now? How will I be able to keep up-to-date on what is happening?

* In this change, am I being singled out or picked on? Will others regard this as discrimination or favouritism?

Supervision

* Will this change mean that I shall be working for a new boss? How will he compare with my present one? How will his expectations be different? What will he consider to be especially important? How will we hit it off together?

* In the new situation, will I be seeing as much of my boss as before? Can my future performance be judged fairly? How will I feel about being left to myself more often?

* In the new situation, will I be seeing my boss more often than before? Will he be looking over my shoulder constantly? How will I feel about that?

* Why was I chosen to try out the change?

Subordinates

* What will my subordinates think of me as a consequence of this change? Will they alter their regard for me? Will they see this as an increase or decrease in my status?

* What kind of new subordinates will I have working for me? How will they compare with my present group? Will we be able to develop as good a rapport? What influence will they have on how effective a job I can do?

Outside contacts (customers, vendors, suppliers, etc.)

* How will those outside the company regard me after this change? Will I be able to get their cooperation to the same extent as now? Will they bypass me and work with others in the company because of this change?

* Will my success in this new territory be as good as the success I've had to date? How difficult will it be to establish new contacts?

* Will my outside contacts regard this change as an increase or decrease in my status in the company? How will my position in my community be affected?

The individual in relation to the organization

* How will my long-term future with the company be affected by this change? How will my chances for advancement be affected? How have others fared in this or similar circumstances?

* How will my future security with the company be affected by this change? Will I be more vulnerable to redundancy? In case of redundancy, what alternative positions might be open to me?

* How important does the company regard this new situation? To what extent will they be watching me? How much is at stake on how good a job I make of it?

* Does the company have as much faith in me as before? How will my new responsibilities and freedom to act really compare with before?

* How does this situation compare with what I might have been able to secure elsewhere? Perhaps I might be able to do better with another company?

Many of these questions will arise out of a genuine conflict of interest. Some, however, may not be realistically based. These would be products of an apprehensive imagination. For the manager, such a distinction is somewhat irrelevant. What is important is that these questions exist and are real for the individual to whom they have occurred. So long as he thinks of them as genuine problems, they must be dealt with in a positive manner by management.

The Manner of Change

Finally, the manner in which a change is introduced and implemented is also an influence on the attitudes of those involved towards it. The effects of how a change is brought about may be quite independent of the effects generated by the change itself. The former depend on how those involved regard the methods employed by management to achieve the desired changes in their behaviour. Any negative attitudes thus generated are most typically directed against the change itself and not against the manner of its realization.

Whenever management institute a change, the number of orders given to subordinates increases substantially. Such an increase in the extent of direction can be, in itself, a cause for resenting the change. Many people resent taking any orders. Others adjust themselves to a degree of control by management, but may become upset when this degree of control is increased. Furthermore, some people, once they have become expert in their jobs, require very little supervision. They often regard this state of affairs with satisfaction and pride. When changes are instituted, these people are subjected to unaccustomed pressures and orders, not only from their immediate supervisors but also from staff specialists and senior management. In such circumstances, these people tend to lose their feelings of autonomy and self-sufficiency. Thus, their dependence on management becomes emphasized, and their resentment of the change can become heightened.

The manner in which a change is instituted can be an influence on people's attitudes towards it in other ways as well. One of these is the extent to which the orders for the change appear to be arbitrary and unilateral. When people feel they must alter their behaviour without any apparent reason, they are likely to be more stubborn in their opposition. Moreover, the feeling that a change is being imposed in a dictatorial manner can also result in hostile attitudes. When a change is brought about in this way, those affected will tend to feel little sense of responsibility for its success.

Additionally, there will be problems if a change is presented as irreversible and irrevocable. Should those affected believe that they are being made to travel down a one-way road and to cross a bridge that will then be burned behind them, their suspicions and fears about the change will inevitably rise.

Furthermore, insufficient information about the change and its probable effects and implications can cause those involved to become apprehensive. When someone's mind is filled with unanswered questions about a change and how it might affect him, he is likely to invent answers to these questions. Whatever he invents will result from his own imagination, hopes and fears. Often, he will come to believe that these invented answers are factual. Typically, such self-developed 'facts' can cause him to become even more suspicious and fearful of the change than he might otherwise have been.

Also, when the people affected are not considered as individuals and are instead treated as an undifferentiated group, category or class, they can resent the apparent lack of concern for and recognition of their individual needs. This resentment can find a ready outlet in negative and resistant feelings towards the change. There is considerable research evidence to support this need for individual treatment.

> Consistently, in study after study, the data show that treating people as 'human beings' rather than as 'cogs in a machine' is a variable highly related to the attitudes and motivation of the subordinate at every level of the organization. The extent to which the superior conveys to the subordinate a feeling of confidence in him and an interest in his on-the-job and off-the-

job problems exercises a major influence upon the attitudes and performance goals of the subordinate.[1]

Finally, the timing of a change can be a source of difficulty. Most of us require time to adjust to a new situation. Time is necessary for us to adjust our thinking to the new conditions. When sufficient time is not allowed for such adjustments, those involved in a change could become bewildered or apprehensive, and develop feelings of opposition.

There is a common root to most of these reasons why the manner of change might adversely affect people's attitudes. This root is the effect of the manner of change on people's fundamental need to feel a sense of importance and personal worth. There is considerable evidence to support the concept that subordinates in an organizational situation react favourably to experiences which they feel support and contribute to this sense of importance and personal worth, and that they react unfavourably to experiences that are threatening to decrease or minimize their sense of importance and personal worth.[2] When a change is introduced in a manner that serves to increase the amount of direction and control on those affected in an apparently arbitrary and unilateral way with little or no explanation and involvement, and when the change is apparently being imposed irrevocably with no seeming concern for their needs, the people who must carry out the change can scarcely escape the feeling that their sense of importance and personal worth is being threatened and reduced. It should be no surprise, then, if they respond with hostile and resistant feelings.

Therefore, the manner in which a change is introduced and implemented can be in itself a source of difficulty. In chapters 6 and 7 we shall discuss in greater detail the significance of this problem, together with its possible solutions.

Attitude Determinants and Resistant Feelings

We have described seven factors that interact to determine how an individual feels towards a change that is about to affect him. His predisposed feelings about any changes and his feelings of personal security are both functions of his own background of experience

[1] R. Likert, 'A motivational approach to a modified theory of organization and management', *Modern Organization Theory* (ed. M. Haire), Wiley, New York, 1959, p. 187.

[2] G. Argyris, *Personality and Organization*, Harper, New York, 1957.
J. G. March and H. A. Simon, *Organizations*, Wiley, New York, 1958.

and of his personality. The existing cultural beliefs and behavioural norms, the patterns of trust and the historical context are all functions of the organizational situation and environment. His reactions to the specific change itself and its manner of introduction and implementation are the product of whatever conflicts and harmony are generated between his interests and those of the organization. How, then, do these factors interact and combine to form the individual's overall feeling towards a change?

We know of no way to describe precisely the interrelationship of these factors. Nevertheless, we can employ mathematical concepts to help make them more clear. We should emphasize from the outset, however, that any mathematical expression we may construct will be inexact. Yet, it can be regarded as giving some indication of the way in which these factors interact and combine.

In considering the seven factors already described, we could say that five of them tend to vary directly with feelings of resistance. That is, anyone's resistant feelings will be more intense when any of the following is greater: (a) the extent to which his predisposed feelings about any change are apprehensive and fearful; (b) the extent of conflict between those cultural beliefs to which he subscribes and what is to be changed; (c) the number of specific unanswered apprehensions that occur to him about how he might be affected by the change; (d) the number and importance of those past historical events that might cause him to be prejudiced against the change; and (e) the extent to which his feelings of self-importance and self-worth are threatened and reduced by the manner in which the change is being introduced and implemented.

Furthermore, some of the other influencing factors tend to vary inversely with feelings of resistance. That is, anyone's resistant feelings will be less intense when any of the following is greater: (a) the extent to which he feels personally secure; (b) the extent of his trust in management, in his union and in his work group; (c) the number and importance of those historical events that might cause him to be prejudiced in favour of the change; (d) the number of his specific hopeful expectations that are confirmed about how he will be affected by the change; and (e) the extent to which the manner of instituting the change contributes to an increase in his feelings of self-importance and self-worth.

Also, we know that some of these factors tend to exert an influence on the intensity and significance of some of the others. For instance, anyone's predisposed feelings about changes in general would probably pervade all his thoughts and feelings about any particular change. The more fearful and apprehensive a person is about changes of any kind, the more he would tend to feel intensely fearful and suspicious towards, and to have a greater number of questions about, a particular change. He would probably interpret every available bit of data in the most pessimistic and negative terms possible.

Likewise, anyone's sense of personal security and feelings of trust would tend to pervade his interpretations of past events that are prejudicial in favour of the change, his hopeful expectations of any benefits that he might gain from the change, and his general satisfaction with the manner in which the change is being carried out. When an individual's sense of security and trust are considerable, he would tend to place an optimistic interpretation on the significance of events, both past and present, as well as amplifying the benefits he might hope to realize.

Finally, because they are both functions of the individual's basic personality and a product of his early experiences, his predisposed apprehensiveness about any change and his personal sense of security tend to be relatively fixed or constant by the time he has become an adult person.

We can see all these direct and inverse relationships together in Fig. 1. When we study this way of expressing these relationships, we can see that:

* Each component of the expression relates to attitudes and feelings. Therefore, the expression as a whole must add up to an overall attitude or feeling.

* Resistant feelings will be intense when the factors appearing in the numerator of the expression are great and the factors appearing in the denominator are small.

* Resistant feelings will be reduced by strong feelings of personal security and trust even though the magnitude of the factors in the numerator might be large.

* The factors that exert the greatest influence on resistant feelings are a person's predisposed feelings about any change, his general sense of security and his feelings of trust. If he is generally apprehensive, this would increase the influence of all the other factors in the numerator. If he should be more confident, this would tend to reduce the influence of all these factors. Similarly, if he

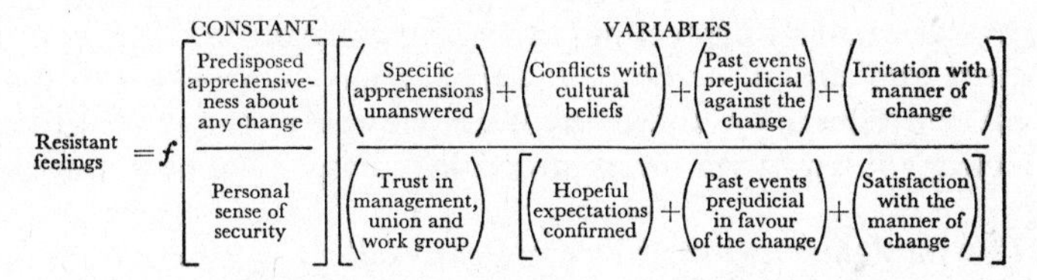

Fig. 1. Relationships between resistant feelings and those factors which are an influence on attitudes towards a specific change.

has strong feeings of personal security and/or trust, these would increase the influence of all the other factors in the denominator, and therefore reduce resistant feelings.

* Clearly, management can have no influence over anyone's predisposed feelings about changes, or over his general sense of security. Furthermore, because trust is the product primarily of the opportunity for interaction, historical development and personal experience, management could do little to alter the established feelings of trust that would be in existence at the time they were about to institute a change. Given sufficient time, however, they could alter these feelings. Finally, management have little control over the influence of historical events relevant to the change.

* At the time of any particular change, management have full control over the influence of only two factors. One of these is the extent to which conflicts between the interests of the people involved and those of the organization are rationalized, and how many of, and how effectively, their questions about their unknown futures are answered. The other is the manner in which the change is introduced and implemented.

* Management can exert limited control over the influence of two other factors. One is the apparent conflicts with prevailing cultural beliefs. The other is the way in which apparently relevant historical events are interpreted.

* Any change might be implemented successfully despite little concern for the human implications provided that the people

involved had strong feelings of security, or trust in their management and union, or both. If this change then proved to have adverse effects on those involved, however, their subsequent feelings of trust with respect to future changes would be lessened.

* The implementation of a change can fail despite active concern by management for those affected. Such a failure could occur if those involved were exceptionally apprehensive about changes in general, personally insecure, if they had little trust, or any combination of these.

Hypothetically, if we could assemble sufficient and accurate data about each of the constants and variables appearing in our mathematical expression we could then estimate the intensity of an individual's resistant feelings. Such a possibility, however, is remote. Not only would we have great difficulty in collecting accurate data, but also we would find these factors extremely difficult to measure and quantify.

Although our mathematical expression should in no way be regarded as a precise statement, it is useful for dramatizing how the seven factors that have an influence on attitudes interrelate with one another and result in an overall feeling about a particular change. It has little use, however, in helping us to predict how people will actually behave. As we shall discuss in the following two chapters, behaviour is influenced by other factors in addition to the ones already described. Nevertheless, we shall point out why and how an understanding of these relationships can help management to reduce or minimize resistant behaviour.

One final point should be made. Attitudes towards any change are based primarily on those assumptions and inferences that a person makes when he imagines himself working in the new situation and under the future conditions. No one, however, can know beforehand with certainty about the precise nature of his working situation after a change. Likewise, no one can know what his new status will really be in these altered circumstances. He must, therefore, make certain assumptions and inferences so that he can provide for his future security.

Whether or not these assumptions and inferences are correct is somewhat irrelevant. To the extent that the individual believes them to be correct he will act upon them. He will continue to act upon these assumptions until his beliefs about his future status are changed.

Summary

Anyone's attitudes towards a change are the consequence of at least seven factors that interrelate and interact in a complicated way:

* *His predisposed feelings about changes of any kind.*

* *The extent of his feelings of insecurity.*

* *Any prevailing cultural beliefs and norms that might be in conflict with the change.*

* *The extent of his trust in his management, his union and his work group.*

* *Objective historical events relevant to the change.*

* *His specific apprehensions and expectations about the particular change.*

* *The manner in which the change is introduced and implemented.*

Because each situation and each individual involved are unique in their characteristics, no formulae can be applied to predict how a particular change will be regarded by those affected. Nevertheless, a manager must understand the nature and source of the factors that shape personal attitudes before he can anticipate with any success their probable attitudes towards a specific change. The identification of such probabilities is a necessary preliminary step for any manager in his planning for the introduction and implementation of that change.

4

How People React to Changes

But men may construe things after their own fashion,
Clean from the purpose of the things themselves.

WILLIAM SHAKESPEARE

If the changes that we fear be thus irresistible, what remains but to acquiesce with silence, as in the other insurmountable distresses of humanity? It remains that we retard what we cannot repel, that we palliate what we cannot cure.

DR. SAMUEL JOHNSON

UP TO this point, we have been concerned primarily with attitudes: how changes tend to generate predictable questions in people's minds, and what are the factors that combine to form their attitudes towards a particular change. But attitudes cannot necessarily be equated with actual behaviour. Before we examine this relationship, let us first consider behaviour itself: what are the various ways in which people can act when confronted with changes. Then, in the following chapter, we shall discuss the relationship between attitudes and behaviour, and to what extent and how it might be possible to forecast, in general, reactions to a particular change, so as to minimize resistance to it.

Spectrum of Possible Behaviour

Individual and group behaviour can range within a broad spectrum of possibilities. At one extreme is active resistance; at the other is enthusiastic support for the change (see Fig. 2). Previously, we noted that anyone's assessment of his future status is influenced by his fears, desires, suspicions and beliefs. To ensure that his apprehensions will not 'come true', the most immediate and obvious action that he can take is to protect and defend his present (and known) status. He does this by resisting the change.

This resistance may take many forms. The particular form depends on the individual's personality, on the nature of the change itself, on his attitudes towards it and on forces deriving from the group and from the organization and its environmental context. Whatever the form of resistance, all types of opposition are a kind of aggressive or hostile behaviour.

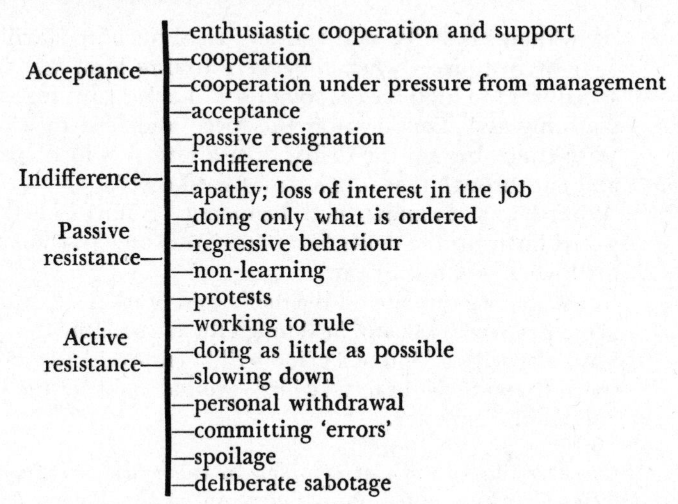

Fig. 2. The spectrum of possible behaviour towards a change.

Frustration and Aggression

The relationship among aggressive behaviour, feelings of aggression and frustration has long been a known psychological concept.[1] Any of us could become frustrated if our personal desires and needs came into direct conflict with external forces which acted to deny these desires and needs. If an individual believes that the future consequences of a change will conflict with his present desires and needs, he will develop feelings of frustration. This frustration, in turn, will give rise to aggressive feelings. Often,

[1] J. Dollard, L. W. Doob *et al.*, *Frustration and Aggression*, Yale University Press, New Haven, Connecticut, 1939.

these feelings are directed towards the source of the frustration. Sometimes, however, they are deflected towards other points. In some instances, the individual might even turn his aggressive feelings inwards, against himself.

Anyone involved in a changing situation could become frustrated. In their most extreme form, his aggressive feelings could find release in active punitive behaviour towards some element of the change. This behaviour could take the form of sabotaging the change by deliberate means. In the following case there is a description of how a drill press operative was successful in resisting the establishment of tighter time-standards on his job.[1]

> 'Ray knew his drills,' said Starkey. 'He'd burn up a drill every four or five pieces when they were timing him, and say the speed was too high for the tough stuff he was running. Tough stuff, my ass! They'd lower the speed and feed to where he wasn't burning up the drills, then afterwards he'd speed up and cut through that tough stuff like cheese.'
> 'What I want to know,' said Tennessee, 'is how in hell could Ward burn up the drills like that? You can't just burn up a drill when you feel like it.'
> 'It's in the way you grind the drill,' said Starkey. 'Ray used to grind his own drills, and he'd touch them up before they timed him. The wrong kind of a grind will burn up a drill at a lower speed than the drill can take if it's ground right for the job.'
> 'Oh,' said Tennessee.

Increasing the amount of spoilage in the work, slowing down the pace of working and committing unintentional 'errors' are all overt evidence of aggressive behaviour directed towards changes. A more subtle means of sabotaging a change might be the practice of following orders in the most literal fashion, or working to rule.

> A new machine was introduced into a manufacturing operation. It was intensely opposed by all the operatives on the shop floor. An engineer was supervising the trial runs and a maintenance fitter from the shop was assigned to assist him. When carrying out orders to make certain specific adjustments on the machine, the fitter noticed that several vital bolts had worked themselves loose. He did nothing about the matter because he had not been so instructed. During the next trial

[1] W. F. Whyte, *Money and Motivation*, Harper, New York, 1955.

> run, the machine became so badly damaged that it was withdrawn from the shop for extensive redesign.

Sometimes, an individual will resist a change by withdrawing entirely from the situation. His absenteeism might increase. Or he might actively begin to seek a change of job. In extreme cases, he might even leave the organization.

Resistance to changes can take passive as well as active forms. Regression to less mature levels of behaviour is one possible outlet for feelings of frustration. We are familiar with the three-year-old child who resumes his thumb-sucking when a new baby arrives in the family. Similarly, a manager, faced with a difficult and complicated change, might find himself unable to make any decisions at all. Or a clerk might find it extremely difficult to learn certain new office procedures. In some cases of frustration, a person might give up trying altogether and become indifferent, apathetic, passive or resigned.

There are other outlets for feelings of frustration. A person might direct his aggressive feelings towards others who are not directly involved in the change. He might become a disruptive influence in his work group by picking on members who are more weak and defenceless. Or he might direct his aggressive behaviour towards members of racial or religious minority groups. Another possible way of behaving might be to become fixated on some useless activity, just as Lady Macbeth became absorbed with washing her hands repeatedly. Thus, to avoid facing a difficult change, a frustrated manager might involve himself in a meaningless task such as reorganizing his filing system.

Another possible consequence of the frustrations caused by a change is that the person affected might direct his aggressive feelings inward, against himself. The result might be a psychosomatic illness such as high blood pressure or ulcers.

> Once we observed a group of working supervisors who had been strongly pressured to increase production under difficult circumstances with no backing from management. There were nine men regularly assigned to the day shift. One had a nervous breakdown, another had a fatal heart attack that was generally attributed to overwork and fatigue. Of the remaining seven, five had serious illnesses and in most cases no organic cause could be determined. All this happened during a period of twelve months. Meanwhile, the men on the night

shift, where pressure was much less, had an almost perfect health record.[1]

Finally, a person might turn away altogether from the source of his frustration by sublimating his aggressive feelings. He might lose all interest in his work and become passionately involved in gardening, local politics or in some other activity entirely apart from his work.

Perhaps these latter forms of resistant behaviour are less immediately damaging than sabotage to the success of a change. Nevertheless, they can diminish significantly the extent of that success.

Organized Resistance

So far, we have been discussing individual behaviour. When a group of people is affected by a change, the intense reactions of some of its members might have an inflammatory effect on the others. This could happen despite the likelihood that many of these members will have relatively mild feelings of frustration. Nevertheless, the majority would be stimulated by those personal fears and dire predictions voiced loudly by the few 'hotheads'. When fears and predictions are infectious, the group often unites and resists the change in an organized manner. Those less inclined towards aggressive behaviour would tend to rally around the leadership provided by the more actively hostile members.

Another reason for organized resistance to changes is that each individual's need for self-protection, so likely to be stimulated by a change, can find its fulfilment in group action. Banding together in a group to resist the change offers people who share this need for self-protection an effective means for ensuring their future security. In its result, this means is often more successful than if each person were to resist separately.

We are all familiar with this phenomenon. One example is the limitation of output by group agreement so that any attempts to increase work standards can be defeated. Another instance is group action to cover up mistakes made by members in their implementation of new work procedures or quality standards. Also, a group might act to withhold vital information from management so that they can be kept in ignorance of what is really happening in a changing situation.

Sometimes, the union will provide leadership for organized

[1] G. Strauss and L. R. Sayles, *Personnel, The Human Problems of Management*, Prentice-Hall, Englewood Cliffs, New Jersey, 1960.

resistance to a change. It will do so if it believes that the interests of its members will genuinely be threatened or damaged by the change. The union might also act, however, if it believes that the change, or the manner of its introduction or implementation, will in some way damage the union's future status. It should be remembered that, although any union is formed originally as a self-protective device for its members, once formed, it becomes an organizational entity. As such, it exhibits a typical characteristic of any organization: the need to survive and maintain a homeostatic equilibrium with its environment.

Every union has its own institutional requirements that must be fulfilled if it is to continue its existence by retaining the loyalty of its members. One of these requirements is recognition by the company of the union's power and status. If management are careful to recognize this fact by discussing its plans in advance with the union, the union might then be more willing to cooperate in the introduction of the change. If, on the other hand, management ignore or bypass the union, it will inevitably oppose both management and the change so that its status will be preserved.

Another area of particular concern to a union is maintenance of its membership. Consequently, changes of special interest to unions are those that impinge on or threaten those employees' rights normally associated with length of service with the company. The union should be involved in discussion of these matters early in the introduction of the change. If this is not done, there will tend to be organized resistance to the change, led by the union.

Acceptance of Changes

Just as there is a variety of behaviour in which people can resist changes, so are there also several different ways in which they can be accepting. The most extreme form of acceptance is enthusiastic cooperation. Although rare, this can occur when an individual's own desires and needs are fulfilled by his expectations about the effects of the change. Even when there are a few minor conflicts between a person's desires and needs and his estimates of the effects of a change, he will still tend to accept that change because less effort is required to accept than to resist.

Group cooperation with a change can be regarded as a kind of defensive action taken by the group.[1] Because the change may be perceived as a threat to the group's stability and continued inte-

[1] R. Dubin, 'Stability of human organizations', *Modern Organization Theory*, (ed. M. Haire), Wiley, New York, 1959, p. 241.

grity, its members may decide that to cooperate with the change is the lesser of two evils. They might believe that to engage in a joint venture is the best method for preserving the group's stability and integrity. They might also believe that failure to cooperate may exclude the group from any potential benefits to be derived, or may even diminish its present 'payoffs' from the organization.

Indifference to Changes

Indifference to a change may be a more common defence against it than is commonly realized.[1] Indifferent behaviour is characterized by two evident manifestations. Sometimes the individual (or group) appears to be ignoring the problems entirely. In effect, he is saying, 'This is really not *my* problem. I shan't be affected significantly'. Alternatively, the individual (or group) may appear to be actively avoiding the pertinent issues by introducing and focusing on subjects that are irrelevant to the problems at hand.

Indifferent behaviour can be a subtle form of resistance. The consequences of such behaviour may affect adversely the successful implementation of a change. Indifference might result in a slowness or difficulty in comprehending the nature of the change and the requirements of the new conditions. The learning of new skills, procedures, etc., would be slowed. Because of the lack of interest, any unanticipated problems resulting from the change might not become apparent soon enough for them to be solved easily. Any potential suggestions from those involved that might be a contribution to the success of the change would be minimized. All these effects would require management to exert more effort and devote more time than might otherwise be necessary for carrying out the change.

Summary

In introducing and implementing changes, the problems of resistance by both individuals and groups are of paramount concern. When resistance exists, it is not so much the change itself that is opposed. Rather, the primary causes for resistance are both the imagined and the real effects of the change on those involved, together with the manner in which the change is being brought about. In reality, the change itself is often only the symbol of what is being opposed.

The key problem in making any change is how to minimize re-

[1] R. Dubin, *The World of Work*, Prentice-Hall, Englewood Cliffs, New Jersey, 1958.

sistance by those involved, in whatever form it occurs. These forms can vary widely, ranging from active outright resistance, through more subtle passive forms including indifference, to acceptance. The manager must be able to anticipate resistance and estimate its intensity. More important, furthermore, he must also anticipate many of its specific causes and reasons. Any manager who does this will then be able to plan and implement countermeasures that should at the very least minimize the resistance and at best transform it into some form of acceptance.

5 Predicting the Extent of Resistance

Change will meet resistance unless it clearly and visibly strengthens Man's psychological security; and man being mortal, frail and limited, his security is always precarious.

PETER DRUCKER

SO THAT appropriate plans can be developed for minimizing any resistance, it is desirable that a manager be able to anticipate how those about to be affected by a change might react. Furthermore, for these plans to be effectively applied, the manager must understand which situational factors he can influence most. Also, he must understand where and how to direct his efforts so that most of the conflicts between organizational and personal needs can be resolved with a minimum of compromise to the desired objectives.

To be able to do all this, a manager needs to know how people form their attitudes towards a change, how they might behave, and what the relationship is between resistant attitudes and resistant behaviour. Moreover, he must grasp the significance of the forces deriving from the organization and group, and their relevance to these attitudes and behaviour. Once he understands the dynamics of how all these factors interrelate and interact, he should then know where his efforts can be applied most productively.

We have already discussed attitudes and behaviour separately. In this chapter, we shall focus on the relationship between the two. We shall also examine further the influence of those organizational and group forces on behaviour. Finally, we shall determine where management must direct their efforts to influence reactions to a change, and we shall then propose an approach whereby these reactions to a specific change can be estimated so that effective plans can be developed for its institution.

A Case of Personal Reactions to a Simple Change

So that the complicated relationship between attitudes and behaviour towards a change might be seen in sharper perspective, imagine that you are in a situation where you are about to be affected by a simple change. How might you feel? How might you actually behave?

Imagine that you are at the opening of a two-day seminar in a city more than two hundred miles distant from your place of business. You have come hoping to learn more about the application of some new long-range planning and scheduling techniques to your business.

Suppose that, prior to your arrival at this meeting, you had received information about the seminar, including a schedule of events. The seminar was scheduled from 9.30 a.m. to 4.30 p.m. on a Thursday and Friday. Each day, there was to be a fifteen-minute break in the morning and again in the afternoon, and a ninety-minute period for lunch. Accordingly, you had arranged to return to your home by a train departing at 5.30 p.m. on Friday.

Now suppose that, during his introductory remarks, the seminar lecturer announces that it will be necessary to alter the schedule. Because there is more material than can be completed within the scheduled time, the length of the seminar must be extended by two hours. Therefore, you are told that the seminar will end each day at 5.30 p.m. instead of 4.30 as previously announced.

If you were in such a situation, how might you feel immediately after such an announcement? There are several possibilities:

1. Damn! I must now catch a later train on Friday. I shall not be able to return home until nearly midnight. I must ring my wife and tell her to cancel our plans for Friday evening.

2. Impossible! I have an engagement I simply cannot cancel on Friday evening. I must leave the seminar before its completion.

3. Good! This is a fine reason for spending the evening here on Friday. I shall ring X . . . whom I have not seen for some time. Perhaps we can get together Friday evening.

4. Good! This seminar may prove even more interesting and valuable than I had anticipated. We certainly seem to be getting value for money.

5. So what? I do not have to be back at any particular time, anyway. I shall arrange a booking on a later train.

6. Hold on! What kind of a seminar is this going to be if the lecturer can't even plan his own schedule properly? I wonder how qualified he is to be handling this subject? I shall certainly listen more critically.

7. Hold on! This is an arbitrary and dictatorial way to make such an announcement. Why couldn't he have consulted us? Perhaps we could work out some compromise in which we might shorten our luncheons and breaks so that we could finish at the originally scheduled time after all.

Any of these attitudes might occur to you. The particular one would depend on your own personality and the extent to which this change either conflicted with or fulfilled your needs and plans at the time. An attitude similar to 1 or 2 might occur if there were conflict. 3 and 4 are examples of attitudes that might occur if the effects of the change to some extent fulfilled your needs and plans. You might feel the indifference of response 5 if there were neither conflict nor fulfilment. Attitudes 6 and 7 would result from irritation with the lecturer's manner of introducing the change.

If any of these feelings occurred to you, how might you actually behave? Just as there are a variety of possible attitudes, so would there also be a variety of possible ways to react. If your attitude were similar to 2, you would be likely to walk out of the seminar before its completion. Attitudes 1, 2, 6 and 7 all involve feelings of frustration and aggression. It is likely that your hostile feelings would be directed towards the lecturer, the source of your frustration. However, the situation is such that you would be deterred from resisting the change directly. In a group of strangers this would be considered unmannerly and impolite. Consequently, you might resist indirectly by becoming inattentive, argumentative during discussions, sceptical about the content of the seminar or a disruptive influence in the group. On the other hand, you might take the initiative and suggest that a compromise in the schedule be considered so that the seminar might end at the originally scheduled time on Friday.

Generalizations from the Case

What generalizations can we make from this simple example that would be relevant to any change in a work situation?

* It is possible that anyone when faced with a change might react by resisting it.

* If you were confronted with a change your feelings might differ considerably from those of the others involved.

* Your behaviour might also be quite different from that of the others.

* Your behaviour might differ even from those with attitudes towards the change similar to your own.

* The extent to which you might resist the change (or vent your hostility on the lecturer) would depend in part on the extent of conflict between your expectations about the effects of that change and your own needs and desires at the time.

* The action that you would *like* to take would depend on the intensity of your feelings and the kind of person you are.

* The action that you actually would take would be influenced both by your desired action (see above) and by your reaction to the pressures exerted on you by the group and by the seminar situation. These pressures would force you towards mannerly and polite behaviour, both with respect to the seminar lecturer and to the others in the group. If they were strangers, this pressure towards polite behaviour might be stronger than it might be if the group consisted of your colleagues (because you might be less concerned with the latter's reactions). In any event, this pressure towards behaving in a socially graceful manner would probably cause you to modify your desired behaviour. In this way your actual behaviour would tend to be a rationalization of your desire to behave in a certain way and your desire to conform to the norms of such a group and situation.

* Suppose that you should resist this change (which is but a trivial aspect of the seminar as a whole). It is likely that, as a result, you would then benefit less from the semiar tha you might other-

wise have done, even though its content might have been of value to you. Thus, from the lecturer's viewpoint, a brilliantly conceived presentation of considerable potential benefit would fail to achieve its intended result. This failure would be caused by the poor handling of a relatively trivial detail, the change in schedule. Therefore, any change with objectives that are sound and justified can fail if the manner in which it is introduced and implemented is mishandled.

* To what extent can we compare this experience of change at the seminar with the experience of any change in a work situation? The two situations are quite analagous, except in one important respect. In the seminar, if the conflicts created by the change were sufficiently intense, you would always have the option of walking out of the situation with little concern for the consequences. At work this method of solving the problem would create new problems far more serious than those presented by the change. Therefore, because the option of walking out is not one that can readily be used by anyone facing a change at work, and because he would probably feel himself somewhat trapped, his feelings of frustration and aggression would tend to be even more intense than those of his counterpart at the seminar.

Organizational and Group Influences on Behaviour

In the case just discussed, we suggested that there were certain group pressures that might have a significant influence on actual behaviour. Just how these pressures appear to fit into the relationship between attitudes and behaviour with respect to a change is hypothesized in Fig. 3.

Thus, we see that although an individual might have the desire to act in a certain way with respect to a change which is to affect him, the way he actually behaves may in fact be quite different. He is reacting not only to the change but also to the pressures exerted on him by the group of which he is a member and by his organizational environment. We should also note that, just as the nature of the individual's personality affects some of the factors influencing his initial attitudes towards the change, so too does the nature of the organization and the group affect some of the other factors influencing his initial attitudes. Finally, we should recognize that anyone's attitudes towards a change after it has been implemented may differ from how he regarded it beforehand. His new attitude will derive from his actual experience of the change, and from his rationalizations about his actual behaviour with respect to that change.

What, then, are the sources of these organizational and group pressures? There is considerable evidence that there are a number of forces stemming from the organization and the group. These forces combine to modify the actual behaviour resulting from the

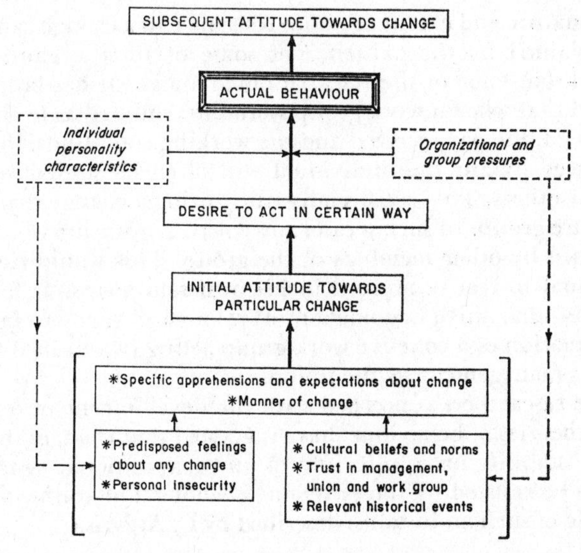

Fig. 3. Attitudes, organization pressures and behaviour with respect to a change.

variety and range of individual desires to act in particular ways in any given set of circumstances.[1] Such objective realities as the nature of the organizational and group structure (its size, design, shape, function, etc.), the kind of managerial controls operating, the technology and organization of the work, the manner in which jobs are constituted, the communication system, the organizational policies, procedures and practices, and the nature of the pay system . . . all these require people with different personalities, needs and goals to behave in a similar manner.

[1] For example, see:
C. Argyris, *Personality and Organization*, Harper, New York, 1957.
C. Argyris, *Executive Leadership*, Harper, New York, 1953.
L. Sayles, *The Behaviour of Industrial Work Groups*, Wiley, New York, 1958.
Work of the Technology Project at Yale University, New Haven (Connecticut).

For example, in one research study, ten supervisors with markedly different personality patterns were found to behave similarly when they were in the plant manager's office. In another study, it was found that there were apparent similarities in behaviour of more than 200 work groups doing the same type of work in the same technological environment in different plants and companies.

The nature and extent of group resistance to a change can partly be explained by the existence of some of these organizational forces. From some of the research noted above,[1] it has been hypothesized that when a work group is undifferentiated as to the tasks performed, the pay received and the working conditions, the problems faced by any one individual will often be similar to those faced by others. This is especially true during a change that affects the entire group. In such a case, any voiced sentiments would soon be echoed by other members of the group. This would cause the individual to feel reinforced in his own sentiments. It has been suggested that this phenomenon of 'resonance' seems to facilitate the formation of a cohesive work group acting in a unified fashion towards management or the union.

Some researchers concerned with the development of organizational theories of behaviour[2] have suggested that changes threatening the stability or equilibrium of an organizational system will tend to be resisted by the system as a whole. The following is an example of such an instance described by C. Argyris.[3]

> In a manufacturing organization, it was found that both the skilled and the non-skilled employees had several 'high potency predispositions' in common: the need to experience (a) togetherness in relation to fellow workers; (b) wages which ensured a fair standard of living and a secure job; (c) non-involvement in the formal activities of the organization, and concern only for their own specific jobs; and (d) control over their own immediate work environment. The foremen in this organization realized that the best way to achieve high productivity, a low rate of grievances and low absenteeism was to maintain the informal employee culture and not to behave in

[1] L. Sayles, *The Behaviour of Industrial Work Groups*, Wiley, New York, 1958.

[2] M. Haire, C. Argyris and E. W. Bakke, for example.

[3] C. Argyris, 'Understanding human behaviour in organizations', *Modern Organization Theory* (ed. M. Haire), Wiley, New York, 1959, p. 150.

a way that violated its norms. Thus, most of the foremen tended to adopt roles that were not directive but rather passive. They concentrated on keeping everyone busy with work that was fairly distributed and that ensured them a fair take-home pay. Otherwise, they left the employees to themselves as much as possible. As a consequence, both morale and productivity were considered to be very high by senior management. At the same time, however, because of the foremen's passivity, management tended to evaluate them as being of a rather low calibre.

Management then introduced a new budget system so that costs could be controlled more rigorously. The introduction of this system caused new pressures to be applied by management to the foremen so that production goals would be raised, piece-rates tightened, informal employees' activities with regard to the incentive system eliminated, etc. These pressures forced the foremen to increase their interaction with both the employees and more senior management, with the aim of 'tightening up' their control. Because the resulting increase in supervisory direction would have disturbed the existing cultural norms, the foremen, realizing this, resisted passing the pressure from the budget system along to their employees. But they could not resist the budget system and their management openly. Instead, they complained about the difficulties and complexities of the budget system, and excused their failure to implement it.

Furthermore, because management held their foremen in low esteem, they tended to delay the effective operation of the new system, thereby making the change easier for the employees. Thus, any excuses offered by the foremen about the complexity of the system and the need for more time to introduce it were generally accepted by management. This, in turn, tended to lower the foremen's aspiration level as to the time for instituting the change, as well as to the extent of change necessary. In this way, the entire organizational system tended to resist a change that was threatening to disturb its equilibrium.

Because organizational and group forces are important influences on individual behaviour, how can we take them into account in our efforts to anticipate reactions to a change? Where should we focus our attention? On behaviour? On attitudes? On what else?

Attitudes, Behaviour and Managerial Influence

At this point, the reader may find himself somewhat confused. He may concede our hypothesis of a complicated dynamic relationship involving individual and group attitudes and behaviour, and organizational forces. He may understand the nature of the interactions and relationships illustrated in Fig. 3 (p. 53). But he may be wondering how he can apply this understanding to the way he introduces and implements a change. More specifically, he may be questioning how this understanding can help him anticipate people's reactions to a change so that he can take these into account in his planning, thereby improving his chances for minimizing resistance.

From our discussion of how attitudes towards a change are formed (in chapter 3), it should be evident that the prediction of these attitudes is difficult enough. But to predict the kind of behaviour that might stem from these attitudes would be even more difficult, because to do so requires an analysis of the effects of whatever organizational forces might be in operation.

If we re-examine the relationships described in Fig. 3 (p. 53), we can see that although an initially resistant attitude may result in a desire to resist, the individual concerned might behave in a way apparently inconsistent with the intensity of his desires. Such would be the case if certain organizational forces caused him to suppress or divert his feelings, and thus modify his actual behaviour. In our example of the seminar at the start of this chapter, although some members may have desired to leave the situation, or to react in a hostile manner towards the lecturer, they would nevertheless have modified the way they actually behaved because of the organizational pressures to act in a socially graceful manner. Still, their negative feelings might have been expressed more subtly through resistance to the ideas presented by the lecturer, and by awkwardness in the discussion periods. Thus, the underlying resistant feelings might nevertheless have had a significant effect on the final outcome of the seminar.

Although it is clear that we cannot say that resistant feelings lead directly to resistant behaviour, we can suggest that if, at the outset of a change, the resistant feelings are slight, then there is little support for any subsequent resistant behaviour. It is doubtful that there can be much resistant behaviour when the more basic underlying attitudes are not resistant.

Most importantly, we should emphasize that the manager's objective is not so much the prediction of attitudes or of behaviour. This is but a means to his real objective, that of minimizing resistant behaviour. If there can be little resistant behaviour without resistant attitudes or feelings to support it, then the manager should be able to achieve his objective by *trying to minimize resistant feelings*. Thus, he can focus on the effects of his intended change on these feelings.

How, then, can such feelings be estimated?

Estimating Resistant Feelings

Estimating possible resistant attitudes or feelings can be a useful step in any manager's planning for a change. From his efforts to forecast such feelings, he should be able to spot any potentially serious problems that might arise from the proposed change or from its manner of institution. With such foresight, he can then reconsider his plans, develop alternative means for accomplishing his objectives, or find ways to solve these problems. How, then, might he go about forecasting the attitudes towards a change of those who are about to be affected by it?

Suppose that you were to be confronted with an impending change. Probably, you would expect that as a result of the change you would be losing certain things that you had previously enjoyed. Also, perhaps, you might expect certain new advantages and benefits. Finally, you would have certain feelings about the way in which you were being treated during the introduction and implementation of the change.

Assume, further, that you were able consciously to identify and analyse how you thought and felt you would be affected. You might then be able to assign to each anticipated gain and loss either a positive or a negative value. A positive value would be indicative of some degree of acceptance of the change, and a negative one would be indicative of some degree of resistance. Your overall attitude, therefore, would reflect the sum total of all these positive and negative values. To the extent that this integrated value were negative, you would tend towards resistance, and to the extent that this were positive, you would tend towards acceptance.

Clearly, it would be very difficult for anyone to identify and analyse his own innermost thoughts and feelings. It should be quite possible, however, for a manager to imagine himself in the position of those of his subordinates about to be affected by a change. He should be able to think about this change in the same way as they would do. He should be able to identify those questions which would most probably arise. From his knowledge of each individual, and of the organizational and cultural context in which he is working, the manager should also be able to identify many of the more comon fears, suspicions and hopes.

Checklists to Aid Estimation of Resistance

The following checklists should prove helpful to any manager in his identification of some of the possible anticipated gains and losses from a change. With his intimate knowledge of the situation and of those involved, he should be able to select from these lists the responses likely to occur. Also, he should be able to translate them into more specific terms to suit the circumstances.

These typical responses are arranged according to the principal reasons for resisting and accepting changes.

Possible reasons for resisting changes (Assumed losses: negative values)	Possible reasons for accepting changes (Assumed gains: positive values)
Feared economic losses	*Anticipated economic gains*
* I am being asked to do more work for the same pay.	* I shall be able to earn more money.
* This change will result in a speedup of the work. My pay will be reduced.	* My opportunities for advancement will be greater.
* Fewer skills will be required of me. My pay will be reduced in the long run.	* I shall be able to develop new or additional skills that will enhance my value and increase my opportunities for earning more.
* I shall be losing much of the overtime that I have been getting.	
* My opportunities for advancement will be reduced.	

Possible reasons for resisting changes (Assumed losses: negative values)	Possible reasons for accepting changes (Assumed gains: positive values)
Fears about personal security	*Hopes about personal security*
* The new situation requires me to learn a new technology or new skills. I doubt that I shall be able to do it.	* The security of my job with the company will be increased because I shall be in a higher classification of work.
* I doubt that I shall be able to meet the new standards of the job that will be required.	* The security of my job with the company will be greater because the importance of my work has been increased.
* I shall be held responsible for quality defects or for the control of quality which I may not be able to influence.	* The security of my job with the company will be greater because the competitive position of the company will be stronger.
* The new situation will involve an increase in safety hazards for me.	* My work will be safer because my exposure to injury or other hazards will be reduced.
* This change will make some people redundant. I don't want to lose my job.	
* I shall be more vulnerable to redundancy in the event of future reductions in business activity.	
* I doubt that I shall be able to handle the increased responsibility.	
Fears about increased personal inconvenience	*Hopes of increased personal convenience*
* The new conditions of work will be less pleasant (physical, environment, location, travel, hours).	* My work will be easier.
* The work will be more difficult.	* My conditions of work will be more pleasant (physical environment, location, travel, hours).
* I shall have to work harder.	* I shall not have to work as hard.

Possible reasons for resisting changes (Assumed losses: negative values)	Possible reasons for accepting changes (Assumed gains: positive values)
* This change will interfere with my personal life (different hours. more travel, etc.).	* This change is an improvement in my personal life (more desirable hours, travel, etc.).
* I shall have to change what I have become accustomed to over the years. What is wrong with the way I am working now?	
Fears about decreased job satisfactions	*Hopes of increased job satisfactions*
* This new job will be less interesting.	* This job will be more interesting.
* There is less challenge in the new job.	* There will be more challenge.
* The pressures on me will be greater (or different).	* The pressures on me will be less (or different).
* I shall have less (or more) responsibility.	* I shall have more (or less) responsibility.
* My authority is being reduced.	* My authority is being increased.
* I shall be receiving much more (or less) supervision.	* I shall be receiving much less (or more) supervision.
* This new job is less important than what I am now doing.	* This job is more important than what I am now doing.
* This new job really does not require my qualifications and training.	* This new job will make better use of my qualifications and training.
* This new situation will be very restrictive. I shall have less opportunity to contribute my ideas and suggestions.	* I shall have more opportunity to contribute my ideas and suggestions.
* This will not fit at all into my long-range career plans.	* This will fit nicely into my long-range career plans.

Possible reasons for resisting changes (Assumed losses: negative values)	Possible reasons for accepting changes (Assumed gains: positive values)
Social fears	*Social anticipations*
* I shall lose status.	* My status will be enhanced or improved.
* If I cooperate with this change, the others will think ill of me. My future relationships will be affected adversely.	* My opportunities for social contacts with others on the job will be increased.
* I shall be less in contact with what is going on in the company (or department).	* I shall have increased access to information about what is going on in the company (or department).
* I don't like working by myself. I enjoy working as part of a team.	* I shall enjoy working as part of a group.
* I'm worried about having Y as a supervisor. He has a poor reputation. I doubt that we shall be able to hit it off very well.	* I shall like working for X. He is a good supervisor.
* This change will damage my relationships with my customers (or suppliers or other persons outside the company).	* My contacts with suppliers (or customers or other persons outside the company) will be improved.
* I shall be establishing precedents by cooperating with this change. I shall be committing other people to follow my example.	* I shall enjoy having that group as my subordinates.
* The Union will take a dim view of my involvement in the change. I shall be affecting their relationship with the company.	
* I shall have to leave my old workmates. I like it where I am. I have no desire to have to make new friends.	
* I don't want to cause others to be made redundant.	

Possible reasons for resisting changes (Assumed losses: negative values)	Possible reasons for accepting changes (Assumed gains: positive values)
Irritation with manner of handling the change	*Satisfaction with manner of handling the change*
* I am unhappy about being picked on. They have something against me.	* I'm quite flattered that I was selected to try out this difficult task.
* No one asked my opinion. I could tell them a thing or two.	* It is satisfying to know that my ideas and suggestions are being sought and are welcomed.
* If we go through with this, there's no turning back. I don't like the idea of burning our bridges behind us.	* This change is really pioneering a new method (or field of endeavour). It is exciting to be able to be a part of this effort.
* This is being done in too much of a hurry. I would like an opportunity to think this over for a time.	* It is gratifying to realize that we are being given the full story on this change and that we shall be able to get answers to our questions.
* This change is really unnecessary. I see no reason to change.	* This change is obviously important, and I'm proud to be a part of it.
* Misunderstanding of the reasons for the change and ascribing incorrect motives.	
* I don't like having things rammed down my throat.	
* This idea is no better than what we are now doing. How is it that he is such an expert? How can he know better than me, he doesn't even work here.	
* He has a nerve implying that we've been having an easy time of it up to now. We've been working hard and doing a fine job.	
* This change comes as quite a shock. It has come so suddenly and unexpectedly.	

Possible reasons for resisting changes (Assumed losses: negative values)	Possible reasons for accepting changes (Assumed gains: positive values)
Cultural beliefs	
* This change goes against what I know to be true. Such a change is inconceivable. It will never work.	
* This change is inconsistent with what I believe in.	
* Why should I cooperate with management anyway? This is the thin end of the wedge.	

Estimation Balance Sheet

We have already suggested that it might be possible to forecast the nature and intensity of resistant feelings if one could integrate all of the positive and negative values of the potential gains and losses that might be the consequences of a change for those affected. Any manager can do this by imagining himself in the positions of those about to be affected and applying the preceding checklists to the particular change at hand. For ease of analysis, he could organize the relevant potential gains and losses in the form of a balance sheet, as shown in Fig. 4.

Such a balance sheet could be constructed either for a group of people or for single individuals, depending on how many are to be affected by the change. For this approach to be useful in forecasting individual attitudes, the manager would need considerable knowledge of each individual as a person, together with information about his reactions towards previous changes. A balance sheet constructed for a large group should prove more useful because of the increased statistical probability that certain kinds of reactions are more likely to occur than others, within a population of considerable size.

In either case, such a balance sheet is useful only as a planning tool. It is no substitute for face-to-face discussions conducted with the people affected to get their reactions firsthand after the change has been announced (as we shall discuss in the following chapters). As a planning tool, however, the development of such balance

Resistance		Acceptance	
Estimated losses	Importance	Estimated gains	Importance
Economic		**Economic**	
- - - - - - - - - - -	—	- - - - - - - - - - -	—
- - - - - - - - - - -	—	- - - - - - - - - - -	—
Security		**Security**	
- - - - - - - - - - -	—	- - - - - - - - - - -	—
- - - - - - - - - - -	—		
- - - - - - - - - - -	—		
Inconvenience		**Convenience**	
- - - - - - - - - - -	—	- - - - - - - - - - -	—
- - - - - - - - - - -	—	- - - - - - - - - - -	—
- - - - - - - - - - -	—		
Satisfactions		**Satisfactions**	
- - - - - - - - - - -	—	- - - - - - - - - - -	—
- - - - - - - - - - -	—	- - - - - - - - - - -	—
		- - - - - - - - - - -	—
Social		**Social**	
- - - - - - - - - - -	—	- - - - - - - - - - -	—
- - - - - - - - - - -	—		
- - - - - - - - - - -	—		
Manner of change		**Manner of change**	
- - - - - - - - - - -	—	- - - - - - - - - - -	—
- - - - - - - - - - -	—	- - - - - - - - - - -	—
Cultural beliefs		- - - - - - - - - - -	—
- - - - - - - - - - -	—	- - - - - - - - - - -	—
- - - - - - - - - - -	—		

Fig. 4. Balance sheet of estimated losses and gains from a change.

sheets can help the manager to anticipate and prepare for how people will probably react to the change. Forewarned and forearmed, he should be able to conduct more meaningful and productive discussions. More important, the results of such a preliminary analysis might encourage the manager to reconsider his approach and perhaps even his objectives, and to introduce whatever modifications seem necessary or desirable.

In constructing a balance sheet, the manager should first list as many of the possible gains and losses as he can imagine from his knowledge of the situation and of those affected. Next, he should try to estimate which of the possible reasons for resistance and acceptance might be the most compelling. This might be defined in terms either of the greatest number in the group affected or of the attitudes and values of each individual involved (if the number is very small). The manager might classify each reason he lists according to his estimate of its probable importance (i.e. its intensity, strength or extent shared); any attempt to differentiate among more than three levels would probably be fruitless. He might then note these estimates for each 'gain' and each 'loss' on the balance sheet.

The manager could then determine the extent of overall balance or imbalance of the 'losses' as compared with the 'gains'. He could also identify which 'losses' and 'gains' appeared to be the most significant in their effect on attitudes, and, to a lesser extent, on behaviour.

The manager must then temper his overall analysis of the summarized balance sheet. He must consider how much trust seems to exist in the relationships between those affected and himself, management as a whole, and the union. He must also try to identify the relevant historical events that might prejudice people either in favour of or against the change. Both these factors should tend either to increase or lessen the intensity of resistant feelings.

Using the Balance Sheet in Planning to Minimize Resistance

Thus, even before a proposed change is discussed with anyone affected, the manager can prepare himself to minimize the effects of the more salient problems, to develop 'gains' that will counterbalance those 'losses' which are unavoidable, and to put the most persuasive case possible to the people affected.

How much reliance can a manager place on the validity of such efforts to anticipate reactions? Clearly, any human being's processes of thought and motivation are too complicated and subtle for others to predict their nature with accuracy. At best, any such predictions could be valid only in terms of probabilities, and even so, a considerable margin for error is inevitable. Thus, a manager should have only modest expectations from any predictions.

Nevertheless, their development can be a productive exercise when he is planning to introduce and implement a change, provided that three conditions are met:

* The existing situation (including the relevant organizational forces, the extent of trust in the relationships and the relevant historical events), together with the nature and exent of the intended change, must be defined clearly and specifically.

* When there are only a few people involved, the manager must have considerable knowledge of those to be affected and of their behaviour during previous changes. However, as the number affected becomes greater, the importance of this condition diminishes.

* The manager must approach the estimation and analysis of their probable attitudes towards the planned change in a systematic and thorough manner (similar to the method we have suggested).

Thus, it would seem worthwhile for any manager to attempt to anticipate the likely reactions to an intended change before he makes it known to anyone affected. This estimate will often be more comprehensive and useful if he involves his subordinate supervisors in this exercise (see p. 176). When a systematic analysis is made an integral element in planning for the change, management will be in a position to develop the most effective strategy for presenting their proposals and for discussing them with those affected.

Summary

Management can attain their objective of minimizing resistance most effectively if they first focus their attention on trying to anticipate the reasons for and intensity of resistant feelings and attitudes.

By constructing and analysing balance sheets for groups or for individuals, a manager can develop a more complete understanding of the following:

* *What is likely to be regarded as both potential losses and expected gains from a change.*

* *The extent of these losses and gains.*

* *The relative intensity and importance of the various reasons for both resistance and acceptance.*

* *The extent to which the expected losses outweigh the gains.*

* *Any probable differences in individual reactions to the change.*

However, we must reiterate that even if a particularly perceptive manager made such an analysis it would be incomplete. No one can possibly anticipate every question and feeling that might occur. Furthermore, the accuracy of such analyses and predictions will be limited. Nevertheless, their development should be a useful exercise for any manager, together with his supervisors, as preparation for instituting a change because:

* *All the managers and supervisors concerned would be in a better position to anticipate the reactions of those involved. They would then be able to plan and prepare their approach and strategy, both with individuals and with groups. They would be able to marshal their arguments in the most persuasive manner possible. They would know what facts are needed to dispel any unrealistic fears.*

* *Management would be able to identify those effects of the change that would probably stimulate such negative reactions that these could not be dissipated by explanations or persuasive arguments alone. They could then either modify the change so as to minimize these negative reactions, or develop alternative means for solving the problems created by the change.*

Thus, such preparation should be one of the first steps in any manager's plan to minimize resistance to a change.

6 Minimizing Resistance to Changes: Concepts

No great improvements in the lot of mankind are possible, until a great change takes place in the fundamental constitution of their modes of thought.

JOHN STUART MILL

Resistance to change by those affected is often the single most formidable obstacle to its successful realization. We have already described this obstacle and how it is formed. Also, we have suggested how some of its characteristics might be anticipated. To what extent can management control this obstacle? How can they reduce or minimize it?

In our previous discussions about the nature and causes of resistance, we suggested that management have the greatest control over two aspects of the situation: the number of unanswered apprehensions that people might have about the change; and the manner in which the change is introduced and implemented. To a considerably lesser extent, management might also exert some control over the influence of conflicts with established cultural beliefs and with relevant historical events. We should now be able to postulate more specifically which variables are present in every changing situation, significant in their influence on resistance, and susceptible to control by management. Once we have identified these variables, we should then be able to formulate how a manager might control them in order to achieve a successful change. In this chapter, these variables are identified and described. The following chapter is devoted to a discussion of some methods for their control.

General Concepts

It should be recognized at the outset that resistance to a change is not the fundamental problem to be solved. Rather, any resistance is usually a symptom of more basic probems underlying the particular situation. To focus attention on the symptom alone will achieve at best only limited results. Similarly, taking drugs may relieve temporarily the ache of an infected tooth. But that ache will continue to recur with increasing severity until the tooth is treated by a dentist. Thus, for really effective solutions we must look beyond the symptom that is resistance to its more basic causes.

We have already suggested that it would be unproductive for management to attempt to influence those forces stemming from the people involved. No manager can nor should try to deal directly with those factors that are deeply personal. To do so would require far greater psychological skills than most managers possess. Furthermore, any attempt to alter elements of personality requires the expenditure of a great deal of time and attention for each individual. Clearly, if a manager had the requisite psychological knowledge and skills, it would nevertheless be impracticable for him to attempt this even with a single person. To try this with a group would be almost impossible. Moreover, any manager who might try this even with one individual would be treading on thin ice with respect to the moral considerations involved.

On the other hand, it is quite appropriate and practicable for a manager to focus on those factors in the situation and working environment that might cause resistance. Many of these variables are directly within his power to influence or control. Often, they can be shaped and modified quite readily. In the end, modifying these environmental variables can have a profound effect on the behaviour of many in the situation.

What, then, are these environmental variables? Which are likely to have the greatest influence on resistant behaviour?

Compulsion

Compulsion is a means by which one individual can attempt to influence or control the behaviour of another. In its most primitive form, it involves physical coercion. In a more sophisticated form, it involves the use of threats to the individual's needs or goals. In business organizations, compulsion is represented by the use of authority. What, then, is the effect of the use of authority when changes are being introduced and implemented?

Let us first reconsider some of the traditional concepts of authority. The classical approach to organization and management is founded upon the principal assumption that authority is the central and indispensable means of managerial control. Furthermore, the concept of authority is regarded in absolute rather than in relative terms.

Both of these concepts are incorrect.[1] Authority is only one means of influencing or controlling the behaviour of others. We have already mentioned physical coercion. Another method is persuasion. Finally, there is the form of influence implicit in professional 'help'. This is based on specialized and expert knowledge. A doctor, architect or engineer, for example, can offer his help to a client. It is understood that this help is being place at the client's disposal, to be used or ignored. Nevertheless, such help can have a decided influence on the client's subsequent actions.

Furthermore, we must realize that all these methods of social control are relative and not absolute. In the final analysis, the success of any method depends on altering the ability of others to achieve their goals or to satisfy their needs. A manager can influence or control an individual only when that person is to some extent dependent on him or the organization. Where there is no dependence, there is no opportunity to control. Thus, both the nature and extent of dependence are critical factors in determining how effective is any method of social control, and of authority in particular.

The effectiveness of authority as a means of control depends in large part on the ability to enforce it.[2] Punishment is the means of enforcement. In business, the form of punishment can range between two extremes: compulsory termination of employment, and limiting the opportunities for advancement. However, in an economy where there is almost full employment, 'the sack' is no longer

[1] D. McGregor, *The Human Side of Enterprise*, McGraw-Hill, New York, 1960.

[2] It also depends on the established framework of cultural beliefs and norms. In cultures where deference to authority is the 'normal' response (as in many Far Eastern societies), the use of authority may still be an effective managerial technique. In fact, the failure to use authority would probably create many more serious problems than its use. In the societies of the Western world, and especially in those of the U.S.A. and the U.K., however, this discussion of the limitations of the use of authority is particularly relevant. Nevertheless, attention should be given to the particular culture of the organization in which changes are intended. The extent to which the use of authority should be avoided depends somewhat on the established attitudes towards its use in the cultures both of the organization and of its social environment.

the threat it once was. Also, the use or threat of punishment can result in countermeasures. Employees are often well protected by the power of their union. They can also act directly by limiting their performance or by refusing to accept responsibility. Thus, employees today are far less dependent on their management than they were fifty years ago. This fact tends to place a considerable limitation on the usefulness of authority as a contemporary method of social control.

There is another problem caused by the use of authority in changing situations. When a change is being instituted and implemented, there is an unusual demand for creative thinking, ingenuity and initiative from everyone involved, if the maximum benefits are to be realized. As we shall discuss later, many valuable contributions can be made both by operating personnel and by lower levels of supervision. But in order to elicit these contributions, an environment must be established that provides subordinates with both the encouragement and the freedom to act. The application of authority, however, tends to restrict this freedom to act. It also discourages the generation and contribution of ideas from subordinates. The use of authority, therefore, tends to produce results that are in direct conflict with what is most desirable in changing situations.

Authority is no longer the central, indispensable means of managerial control. Instead, it is the fact of interdependence that characterizes contemporary organizational relationships in business. It is still true that subordinates are to an extent dependent on their managers for the satisfaction of their needs and the achievement of their goals. But it is also true that managers at every level are likewise dependent on all those below them for achieving both their own goals and those of the organization. Furthermore, this interdependence is also a characteristic of the relationships between managers and staff specialists, between 'line' departments, and among any group of individuals who report to a common supervisor. This interdependence becomes especially important during periods of change, when cooperation and teamwork become essential for the success of the change.

Dependency is another problem associated with the use of authority as a method of influence and control in changing situations. The emotional responses relating to dependency are very complicated. Everyone's development from the moment he is born involves the change from being totally dependent on his parents for life itself towards a state of independence as an adult. But at no stage of this development can he be entirely satisfied. Although dependency can be satisfying in the security it provides, it is also frustrating in the limitations it imposes upon the freedom to act as one wishes. Likewise, although independence is satisfying in that one can make decisions for one's self and lead one's own life, it can also be frightening because of the risks involved. Thus, everyone tends to have conflicting emotions about dependency. Many people, when placed in situations which emphasize their dependency, would become frustrated and rebellious.

In any changing situation, the problem of dependency often becomes acute because its extent is increased. The familiarity and comfortable security of the individual's work world disappears. In its place is an unknown future filled with fearful possibilities. To him, the principal point of reference that remains constant is the organization as a whole, and often, but not always, his manager. It is inevitable that he should feel more dependent under such circumstances, because he has lost much of his control over his work situation. Resentment, frustration and resistance are often the consequences.

Thus, in most organizations operating within a 'Western' cultural framework, compulsion through the use of authority as a method for instituting and implementing changes will inevitably increase the frustration of those involved. This will occur because of the additional pressures imposed on them. Their frustration will mount also because of the increased limitations on their freedom to act. Finally, their frustration will grow as a consequence of the increase in their dependency. The inevitable result of this heightened frustration will be an increase in aggressive and hostile feelings. In many instances, the end result will be more resistance towards the change. Therefore, compulsion and the use of authority in managing any change will serve to increase resistance to it.

Persuasion

If authority and the threat of punishment are undesirable elements in a changing situation, what about the use of persuasion and rewards as a means of gaining acceptance and cooperation?

Certainly, persuasion is one means for influencing the behaviour of others. In selling, for example, persuasion is the principal means in use. The essence of this approach is to convince an individual that if he behaves in the manner desired he has much to gain.

Clearly, he will gain more than he might lose. Persuasion, if it is to be successful, depends on the ability to perceive a situation from the other person's viewpoint. A correct analysis of his needs and goals is fundamental. Only after this is done can the potential gains be emphasized and the potential losses be explained away.

In the hands of management, however, persuasion is often not really as straightforward a method as it might seem at first. In selling, the salesman has no further recourse than persuasion. But in management there is often the expectation that authority, or even coercion, might be resorted to if persuasion should fail. Thus, the use of persuasion by managers is often perceived by their subordinates to be something more than simply straightforward 'selling'.

Just as the use of authority depends on the threat of punishment, so does persuasion depend on the offer of promise of rewards. Rewards are most commonly regarded in financial terms. In certain circumstances, the use of financial rewards is essential. This is so when the reasons for resistance are primarily economic.

For example, as a consequence of an impending change, one group of employees might believe that they would have to work harder. Another group, facing another change, might believe that they would have to produce more. Still another group might believe that they were in danger of suffering a reduction in their earnings. We should assume that in each of these situations those involved believed that as a consequence of the change they would have to increase their efforts and contributions to the job. In such circumstances, it is probable that in not one of these cases would the change be acceptable unless those affected believed that they would be justly compensated for their increased effort. Such compensation would have to take the form of increased earnings, or possibly an altered system of wage payment. Thus, when there are economic reasons for resisting a change, financial rewards must be offered if this resistance is to be lessened.

If, however, the reasons for resistance are primarily non-economic, or if there are both economic and non-economic reasons present, the use of financial rewards as the only method of minimizing resistance can create problems instead of solving them. Indiscriminate offers of rewards will often cause serious conflicts for those involved. The following example should illustrate this point.

> John is a skilled machinist working in an engineering firm. In this job, he enjoyed the varied work of operating lathes, mill-

> ing machines, screw machines and the like. He also enjoyed his associations with his workmates. The company purchased an automatic, computer-controlled milling machine. This was installed in a special air-conditioned room, constructed in one corner of the machine shop. John was selected to become the operator of this new machine. To ensure his acceptance, he was offered a substantial pay rise. Although his feelings about the new job were mixed, John felt that he could not afford to refuse the increased compensation. Once on the new job, however, John's feelings about his work changed. He missed the variety in his prior job. He longed for the frequent and friendly interchanges with his associates. He began to feel that his past knowledge and skills were being wasted on his new job. Yet, he felt compelled to remain in his new situation because of the high rate of pay. As a consequence of his increasing frustration, the quality of his work began to decline.

Thus, the use of a monetary reward resulted in a change that was initially successful. But the failure to consider the other problems in the situation eventually caused this success to miscarry.

Conversely, the use of non-economic rewards to persuade individuals to accept a change that may adversely affect their earnings is not only unlikely to succeed, but is also immoral. In their book *Personnel, The Human Problems of Management*, G. Strauss and L. Sayles comment on this point: [1]

> True, an employer may successfully manipulate an employee into acquiescing to a change that is not in the employee's best interest. But in the long run in a free society such attempts at brain-washing tend to backfire against their instigators. We emphasize this point because there are employers who feel that if proper 'human relations' are applied, employees will be willing to do without a fair wage. Such misuse of human relations is, in our opinion, highly immoral; fortunately, it is rarely successful.

When the reasons for resistance are primarily non-economic, persuasion, if it is to be successful as a method of influence, must depend on non-economic rewards. These can take many forms. For example, a change might present opportunities for acquiring new

[1] G. Strauss and L. Sayles, *Personnel, The Human Problems of Management*, Prentice-Hall, Englewood Cliffs, New Jersey, 1960, p. 272.

knowledge and skills. These, in turn, might enhance an individual's worth to the company. Or he might improve his opportunities to advance, or to further his career. Also, there might be opportunities for increases in the security of his job, or in the satisfactions he derives from his work. Certain aspects of the work might become more convenient and pleasant. There might also be improvements in status and in the nature of the social relationships associated with the work.

When the prospect of any of these rewards is used deliberately to persuade others to alter their behaviour, it can often be as effective as the offer of economic rewards. This is true when the nature of the reward is made relevant to the specific reason for resistance, and when the promise of the reward can be realistically fulfilled.

Thus, both the extent and nature of any persuasion used in a changing situation are key variables in determining the success of the change. The effectiveness of persuasion as a means of influencing the behaviour of others depends on the extent to which the rewards offered are both relevant to, and counterbalance and outweigh, the reasons for resistance.

Security

How much one's security is either threatened or ensured in a changing situation is another variable that has both a great influence on resistance and is susceptible to management control.

We have already described some of the reasons why anyone might be apprehensive about his personal security when he faces a change (see checklist, p. 59, and the discussion of feelings of insecurity, pp. 21–22). Some of these apprehensions may be sheer imagination. Others, however, may be based on a realistic appraisal of the situation. The most significant fear is often that of redundancy.

Fears of redundancy can result from any one of several assumptions that a person might make when he faces an impending change. He might assume that his job will be eliminated. Or he might believe that his vulnerability to redundancy will be increased. Or he might fear that he will become redundant because he will be unable to learn or meet any new standards required. Often, the individual's own past experiences of redundancy, together with the history of redundancy in the organization, the community and the region, will be important influences on his fears.

Whatever assumptions are the basis for fears of redundancy, intense resistance to the change can result. Anyone will tend to resist a change if he believes that by so doing he will protect his own interests and preserve his job. Or he might resist in an effort to preserve the jobs of his workmates.

Fears of redundancy can cause not only intense resistance to a change, but also a general deterioration of both morale and performance of work. Such fears can be highly infectious and can affect many in the organization who have no relationship whatsoever to the change. These fears must be removed if resistance is to be minimized. Frank Cousins, while he was leader of the Transport and General Workers Union (the largest union in Great Britain), once made the following comment:[1]

> When workers are told to accept new methods and not be modern Luddites, we have to consider how right in the short run the Luddites were. Machine looms destroyed the jobs of thousands of handloom weavers. They were introduced without consultation, without any regard to human values, and they had dire consequences for the men directly concerned. We can look back 150 years and say there should have been a rapid step into machine operation, but for the people involved they were absolutely correct to resist it, because no one did anything about their side of the problem. We must make it unnecessary for modern workers to think in the same terms and there is some of that thinking still existent. We must give a degree of security which will enable workers to welcome new methods, to allow a degree of flexibility in industry which cannot come until real security is present.

Often, a change represents some threat to the security of those affected. Fears of redundancy, either for one's self or for others in the work group, are often the result. These fears must be dispelled if resistance to the change is to be minimized.

Understanding

How much understanding there is in a changing situation is another variable that is both significant and controllable. In this discussion, we shall consider both what must be understood and who must have this understanding.

[1] F. Cousins, Industrial Relations, A Forward Look, an address made to the British Institute of Personnel Management, October 1962.

The briefest answer to the question of who is everyone involved in the change. Just as the manager must understand what is going on and why, so must those affected understand as well. Likewise, those lower-level supervisors and staff specialists who are essential for implementing the change must have understanding. Also, if there is a union involved, its officials must understand. 'Who' should be defined as broadly as possible. The more widespread there is understanding of all aspects of the change, the less likely there will be resistance.

What, then, must be understood? Everyone involved should know the answers to the following questions, to the fullest possible extent:

* What are the specific long-term objectives to be accomplished?
* What are the specific short-term objectives to be accomplished?
* Why is there a need for these objectives to be accomplished?
* Why is there a need for a change at all? . . . for this change in particular?
* What is to be changed?
* How is it to be changed?
* When is the change to take place?
* Who is to be involved?
* How are those involved to be affected?
* What will the situation be after the change?
* What are the potential benefits that might be gained from the change?

Several points about the above list are important. An understanding of the reasons for the change may require a detailed and specific demonstration that there is a genuine need for a change. To accomplish this, management may need to furnish documentary evidence. Also, the particular means for accomplishing the change should be perceived by those affected as a tentative proposal and not as a final, definite method with an inexorable and inflexible schedule. It must be made clear that there is ample latitude for alterations or modifications to be made later on to the method, if there is sufficient justification. It should be understood that the door is constantly open so that new information and ideas can be incorporated, if these are relevant to the accomplishment of the desired objectives.

Finally, there might be certain factors in a situation that would tend to limit the amount of information that could safely be revealed. One such factor is security, whether it be related to the company, its marketing practices, or perhaps to military or governmental information. A management might believe, for example, that certain information must be kept secret. For instance, knowledge of an impending replacement of an executive might prove disruptive and damaging to morale. Or, knowledge of some new product or marketing strategy might cause the company's competitive position to be endangered or weakened. Or, the leakage of some information might be detrimental to the national interest or security. Sometimes, classifying and treating such information as secret is fully justified. Often, however, expectations of damage resulting from sharing such information judiciously are exaggerated.

Management should view matters of security realistically. They should compare the risks that might be incurred by a leakage of information to the wrong parties with the risks that might be incurred by treating this information as secret. Excessive secrecy can easily lead to misunderstandings which in turn can cause increased resistance to the change. From a deliberate consideration of these comparative risks and the possible consequences, management should be able to decide how much information they should share in advance.

In addition to the material outlined above, managers and staff specialists should develop some understanding of the specific personal attitudes and social arrangements that would tend to be both sustained and threatened by the change and its method of realization. With this knowledge, they should be able to increase their consideration of these factors both in planning and implementing the change. As we shall discuss further in chapter 8, managers and staff specialists often regard changes quite differently from the people affected. If managers and staff specialists are unaware of or insensitive to the effects of a change on existing attitudes and social arrangements, they would tend to overlook certain elements of the change which might affect these adversely. Greater resistance to the change could result.

Finally, if a particular change is in conflict with certain prevailing cultural beliefs (see pp. 23–25), this conflict should be resolved. Resolution depends first on a conscious realization that some conflict actually exists. Because cultural beliefs are based on implicit assumptions that certain institutional practices are necessary, their validity is rarely, if ever, examined or challenged. These assumptions should first be identified. Their validity should then be questioned and reappraised in the light of the existing and the future situation. Through such a process, any potential conflicts between the effects of the change and the prevailing cultural beliefs can be averted.

In an attempt to define an 'ideal' organization with impressive characteristics of performance, R. Likert has suggested that such an organization must have:

> '. . . conditions that lead to full, candid communication. To give relevant information to others and to be interested in and receptive to the relevant information which they have is to behave in a supportive, ego-building manner. To withhold relevant information or to show no interest in information others seek to give us is to behave in a threatening and ego-deflating manner. To give information conveys trust and confidence in others, and increases their sense of personal worth. To withhold information does the opposite.' [1]

There is a direct relationship between how much those involved in a change understand about it and all its implications, and their resistance to it. When as many of these people as possible understand as much as is possible about that change (and in particular about how it will affect them), their resistance to it will probably be lessened. When, on the other hand, little information is made available, a vacuum will be created by the lack of facts. This vacuum will be filled by conjectures and assumptions. In such circumstances, resistance to the change is likely to be great.

Time

Time is a significant and controllable variable in any changing situation. Two periods of time are important: (a) the interval between the first inkling that a change is to occur and its actual start; and (b) the interval between the start of the change and the

[1] R. Likert, in *Modern Organization Theory* (ed. M. Haire), Wiley, New York, 1959, p. 209.

completion of its implementation. What is the relationship between the length of these intervals and resistance?

Consider first the period of time between the moment when the people involved first hear about an impending change and its actual start. Is it better in terms of lessened resistance for this period to be long or short? The answer depends in part on the extent to which management are willing to share and discuss information about the change before its introduction.

Generally, slow changes are less threatening than rapid ones. This is so because we often 'get used to an idea' when we have sufficient time to think about it. Our capacities for adjustment to changing circumstances seem almost limitless. Throughout the past sixty years, for example, most of us have had to make continuous adjustments in our way of life as a consequence of changes brought about by science and technology. These changes were made available, and when we were ready we adopted them. Initially, many may have rejected as outrageous or absurd the ideas of riding in automobiles, or flying in aeroplanes, or eating frozen food, or wearing clothes made from synthetic fibres, or travelling to other planets. Yet, in time, most of us have come to accept these enormous changes. Why is this?

When a new idea is first introduced to us, we begin to think about and consider it from many different viewpoints. In time, its novelty and strangeness disappears. Eventually, it becomes familiar. If we are able to observe the application of this idea to others around us, we can then estimate better how it will probably affect us. If our initial fears are dispelled, we become reassured. We then can absorb the idea and regard it as our very own. Thus, the idea is no longer something imposed on us by some external forces. Instead, it becomes something we have thought about ourselves. This process of self-adjustment has been named 'accommodation'.[1]

Another basis for adjustment to the idea of a change is the process of rationalization. Most of us when faced with the inevitable can be quite inventive in finding a variety of reasons to justify why we should comply with a change. We do this to protect ourselves from the discomfort of conflict and anxiety. Through rationalization, we convince ourselves of the necessity for and soundness of the change.

When people have a long time to think about a change before it affects them, they have ample opportunity to voice their questions and fears. Many of their problems can then be resolved in advance

[1] A. Bavelas, *The Journal of Social Issues* (U.S.A.), **4**, No. 3, Summer 1948.

of the change, in a leisurely atmosphere that is relatively dispassionate. It is also likely that in this process of discussion some useful suggestions might be offered that would improve the approach to the change. Through such discussions people will come to know what to expect. They can then adjust their thinking and attitudes, and become more receptive towards the change.

The longer this interval is between the initial communication about a change and its date of initiation, the greater will be the opportunity for those involved to adjust themselves. On the other hand, the shorter this interval is, the more resistance there is likely to be. Most people tend to react strongly when they feel that they are being compelled to do something before they have had even the opportunity to consider it and to ask questions.

There is, however, an important qualification to this principle. A relatively long time to consider a change before it occurs is desirable only when management can both reveal and discuss freely information about the change and its consequences. When this is not possible, and only the fact of the impending change is made public, a long period between the announcement and the change can actually cause difficulties. People would then have more time to worry and build up hostility and resentment. They would also have more opportunity to organize their resistance.

> A large insurance company was moving its principal office from its original, somewhat antiquated building into a modern steel-and-glass structure. About six weeks prior to the move, an announcement in writing was circulated to all those secretaries and stenographers assigned to individual managers. From this single sheet of paper, the girls learned that after their move to the new building they would no longer be private secretaries and stenographers. Instead, they would be grouped together into a 'pool' to serve any manager requiring secretarial services. No reasons were offered for this change. By the time the move was made, more than 70% of the secretarial staff had resigned for 'better positions' in other nearby offices.

Once a change has been initiated, is it desirable to carry out its realization over a long period of time? Certainly, resistance to a slow change will be less intense at any one time than it would be to a more rapid change. Nevertheless, there are several dangers in prolonging the process. A slow change would cause those affected to make a continuing series of adjustments over a long interval. Thus, the period of personal and social disruption and turmoil would be extended.

Furthermore, it would be difficult for management to ensure that those involved maintain a clear understanding of the overall scope of the change, together with an understanding of all the elements described in the previous section. People would tend to view each increment of the change in isolation, and not as part of a grander design. When those involved lose sight of the ultimate objectives and their justifications, they would probably not understand the significance of each increment of the change. Thus, their questions and apprehensions would tend to multiply.

Finally, a change carried out in a piecemeal fashion would often yield diminished benefits because it would be difficult for management to consider at any one time all the implications and ramifications of the change as a whole. They would be less able to plan effectively. Also, they would probably have increased difficulty in evaluating its results.

The length of time between the announcement of an impending change and its initiation tends to vary inversely with the extent of resistance, provided that information about the change can be shared and discussed freely. That is, the longer the time, the lower the resistance. On the other hand, the length of time it takes for the change to be realized tends to vary directly with resistance: the longer this period, the greater the resistance.

Involvement

Yet another significant and controllable variable in a changing situation is the extent to which those affected are actually involved in making some of the decisions about the change.[1] Most of us gain considerable satisfaction from exercising some control over our working environment. We gain further satisfaction from the feeling of success that results from having accomplished something by ourselves.

As a consequence, most of us would like to take part in making decisions that affect us directly. If this desire were fulfilled, our interest in our work would become heightened. Furthermore, we would be more likely to accept a change to which we might other-

[1] Here again we are assuming an environment where the cultural values are such that the use of authority is generally undesirable and the need for self-realization is relatively strong.

wise have objected. Our perception of this change would be altered. We would no longer feel that something was being done *to* us. Instead, we would feel that this change was being accomplished *by* us, at least in part.

Let us consider several examples of the effects of personal involvement in making changes.

* Industrial engineers in a metal-plating department had been trying for a long time to figure out an equitable way of dividing up the girls' work. The operation was unusually complex and erratic, and every time the engineers made a suggestion the girls were quick to prove that it was unfair to someone. The engineers were about to give up in disgust when the girls asked, 'Why not let us decide?' In a short while they had worked out job allocations that even the engineers agreed were superior to theirs.[1]

* An experiment was made with girls who were learning machine-paced work and who were failing to keep up with the required pace. In discussions with their foremen, the girls requested that they be allowed to determine the pace themselves. A dial was installed that allowed them to set their own speed. It was discovered that the girls established a pattern of work which varied with the time of day. Nevertheless, the average speed was considerably higher than the constant speed previously set by the engineers. Yet, the girls reported that their work was easier. Their total output was between 30 and 50% higher than expected.[2]

* The superintendent of a machine operation was convinced by his safety department that long-sleeved shirts were a safety hazard even when rolled up. So he posted a notice that, beginning the next Monday morning, wearing long-sleeved shirts on the job would be prohibited. Monday morning, four men showed up with long sleeves. Given the choice of working without shirts or cutting off their sleeves, they refused to do either and were sent home. The union filed a sharp grievance, asking for back pay and for time lost. Then the Personnel Department stepped in.

[1] G. Strauss and L. Sayles, *Personnel, The Human Problems of Managerment,* Prentice-Hall, Englewood Cliffs, New Jersey, 1960, p. 166.

[2] W. F. Whyte *et al. Money and Motivation,* Harper, New York, 1955, chapter 10.

> The rule was suspended for a week and a special meeting was called with the union grievance committee. The safety director explained that if a worker got his sleeve caught in a machine his whole arm might be ripped off. The union agreed to the rule providing that it was extended to include management (who had originally been exempt on the grounds that they didn't get close enough to the machines). Next Monday, the rule went back into effect. A few men, forgetfully, arrived in long sleeves. The other men handed them a pair of scissors and insisted that the offending sleeves be cut off on the spot. Later in the afternoon, a union vice-president and a company time-study man were treated in the same way.[1]

Another result of personal involvement in making some of the decisions about a change is that the individual often feels a sense of commitment to carry out his decision. He feels a share of the responsibility. When a group is so involved, even if an individual member has reservations about the decision, he is under strong pressure from others to implement it. This is dramatized vividly in a case which illustrates what happened when workers engaged in the maintenance and repair of furnaces were encouraged to establish their own production goals.

> Groups that participate in setting goals for themselves often make higher demands for themselves than their supervisors and methods engineers consider to be practical. A furnace-cleaning job was cut from four to two days; tardiness was set at less than three per cent when formerly it was ten per cent; service calls were reduced from one in fourteen to one in twenty-one . . . repairs per man per day rose from 8.5 to 12.5 when the crew planned the service; and over a period of three years, men worked more days when they decided whether or not the weather was inclement than when the supervisor made the decision.[2]

Clearly, therefore, the greater the extent of personal involvement in making some of the decisions about a change, the less will be the resistance to it.

[1] G. Strauss and L. Sayles, *Personnel, The Human Problems of Management*, Prentice-Hall, Englewood Cliffs, New Jersey, 1960, p. 168.

[2] N. R. F. Maier, *Psychology in Industry*, 2nd edn., Houghton Mifflin, Boston, 1955, p. 172.

Criticism

Still another significant and controllable variable in a changing situation is the extent to which those involved feel criticized as a consequence of the change.

In any change, there is an implied criticism of the past or present situation. The need to change carries with it a clear implication that there is something wrong or inadequate about the existing circumstances. Otherwise, why should there be a change at all? Sometimes this criticism is perceived as being levelled at lower levels of management and supervision. They may feel some guilt because they did not initiate the change. When it is introduced by their seniors, these managers and supervisors at lower levels may feel that higher management will regard them as lacking in both ingenuity and initiative for not having taken action themselves.

In other instances, the operatives may feel criticized. They may believe that the change was introduced because their work was of an insufficiently high standard, either of quality or quantity. Or, they might perceive a change as an expression by management of little trust in their ability to perform their jobs properly.

Still another case is the new manager or supervisor who introduces changes in operating procedures. His subordinates might interpret his actions as a criticism of their previous boss. Often, their loyalty to the prior man is stronger than it is to the new manager.

When anyone feels criticized, he becomes resentful and defensive. This resentment and irritation is naturally directed towards the source of the criticism, either the change itself or its originator. This irritation and resentment can readily become translated into resistance to the change. Therefore, the greater the feeling of being criticized, the greater is the resistance.

Flexibility

Our last significant and controllable variable in a changing situation is the extent to which those involved perceive the change and its method of accomplishment to be subject to modification.

We have already stated that most people desire to exercise some control over their environment at work. Conversely, when they feel no sense of control and at the mercy of external forces, their feelings of dependency and frustration are likely to increase. The interrelationships among dependency, frustration and resistance to changes have already been described.

When most people are confronted by an impending change which they regard as inexorable and irrevocable, their feelings of helplessness increase. They may feel that it is futile to voice any fears or reservations. Their frustration may be further increased by their view that management have little aparent sensitivity towards or concern for their needs and desires. Their only recourse, then, is to resist.

On the other hand, if an individual believes that he has some influence on the course of the changing circumstances, he will have a constructive outlet for his fears and questions. He will feel that he has some measure of control over his future.

Clearly, therefore, an inexorable and rigid implementation of a change, that makes no allowances for modifications to the methods of its realization, will inevitably provoke resistance. On the other hand, this reason for resistance will evaporate when those affected by the change believe that there is sufficient latitude in the methods of approach for their suggestions and contributions, as well as for any unforeseen factors, to be incorporated.

Summary

There are eight variables in any changing sitation that can be controlled by management and that can cause resistance. By the way in which they use compulsion, persuasion, security, understanding, time, personal involvement, criticism and flexibility of approach, management can remove or reduce the influence of many factors that cause resistance to changes. In the following chapter, we shall discuss some methods of controlling these variables.

7

Minimizing Resistance to Changes: Methods

It is not true, as a good many industrial psychologists assert, that human nature resists change. On the contrary, no being in heaven or earth is greedier for new things. But there are conditions for man's psychological readiness to change. The change must appear rational to him; man always presents to himself as rational even his most irrational, most erratic changes. It must appear an improvement. And it must not be so rapid or so great as to obliterate the psyhclogical landmarks which make a man feel at home: his understanding of his work, his relations to his fellow-workers, his concepts of skill, prestige and social standing in certain jobs and so forth.

PETER DRUCKER

A MANAGER can minimize resistance to any change by focusing on the eight variables described in the previous chapter and exercising his power to control each of them.

Preferably, any resistance should be minimized while it is still potential rather than real. The manager can do this if he incorporates into his plan for accomplishing the change those specific methods he wishes to employ for controlling these variables. Even if the resistance becomes an actuality, however, he should still be able to influence these variables so that resistance is reduced. What methods can a manager employ to control each variable?

Compulsion, Threats and Bribery

Fundamentally, two general approaches are possible for minimizing resistance: increasing the pressures to overcome resistant behaviour, or reducing the very forces that cause resistance. In the first approach, the act of resistance itself is attacked directly. The causes or reasons for the resistance are ignored. Thus, only the symptoms are dealt with.

By using his authority, for example, a manager can threaten his subordinates with disciplinary action or even with 'the sack' if they do not comply with a change. But we have already pointed out that such compulsion could result in immediate countermeasures that would prevent or delay the change from taking place. Or, the change could subsequently be sabotaged to the extent that no benefits would be realized.

Furthermore, we have cited cases to illustrate how indiscriminate offers of increases in pay to bribe subordinates into accepting changes can also fail to produce lasting benefits. When the reasons for resistance are primarily non-economic, such bribes are an attack on the resistance rather than on its causes. Thus, bribery often creates new problems which could eventually nullify any potential benefits from a change.

Therefore, any approach that aims directly at overcoming resistance itself, whether by threats or by bribery, is both unwise and undesirable. The consequences of such an approach will be to reduce rather than to increase the possibilities for successful implementation of a change. The use of either threats or bribery should be rejected outright by any manager in his choice of methods for reducing resistance.

Persuasion, Rewards and Bargaining

The proper use of rewards, together with the other methods for minimizing resistance to be discussed in the following pages, are all means for reducing the forces that result in resistance. By attacking the root causes instead of the symptoms, a manager should improve his chances for bringing about a change successfully.

The proper use of rewards has already been referred to previously. The offer of a reward that is relevant to a specific reason for resistance can be a powerful incentive for accepting a change. Before introducing the change, a manager can identify many of the probable reasons for resistance, and then develop a specific balance sheet of estimated losses and gains for those affected (see Fig. 4, p. 64). From this, he can determine which of the probable losses might be offset by the offer of appropriate compensatory rewards. Also, he can identify which of the possible gains should be emphasized in his discussions with those involved. Used in this way, the offer of relevant rewards should reduce, if not remove, some of the causes of resistance.

We have classified all rewards as either economic or non-economic. Economic rewards lead to greater annual total compensation. Often, an increase in the rate of pay can be justified by the alterations that are made to the content of individual jobs as a consequence of a change (e.g. in terms of increases in responsibility, mental and physical effort required, education and experience needed, etc.). An economic reward can also be in the form of an altered system of wage payment that enables greater earnings, or earnings that are perceived as more equitable (e.g. the introduction or elimination of individual or group incentives). Alternatively, the economic reward can be in the form of 'fringe benefits' such as an improved pension scheme, better holiday or sickness protection plan, or a minimum guarantee to the level of earnings. All economic rewards, whatever their form, are useful to satisfy the feeling by those affected that a desired change somehow increases the value of what they are being asked to do.

The variety of non-economic rewards is considerably greater because the needs they might satisfy range more widely. For example, concern about threats to status might be met with an offer of: a more impressive job title; better perquisites; changing the pattern of personal interactions (i.e. inclusion in certain meetings, on certain distribution lists, etc.); or even training. Reorganizing the way the work is done or resructuring the relationships within a work group might lead to more pleasant social relationships in the work situation, or to the opportunity of gaining greater satisfaction from the work itself. Providing opportunities for training might enhance one's opportunities for personal development within the organization. As with economic rewards, the particular non-economic reward offered must be carefully matched to meet an existing need.

The technique of bargaining is a variation of the use of persuasion through rewards. Bargaining is a process based on discussions between management and those affected by a change and/or their union representatives. In this process, management's objective is to gain acceptance of their proposals. Management in no way are committed in advance to accept any proposals made by the group with whom the discussions are held. There is, however, an implicit understanding that management might accept some of the proposals put forward by the group as a *quid pro quo* in exchange for the group's acceptance of the remainder of what management want. In a sense, then, the concessions or compromises made by management in bargaining are quite comparable to the offer of rewards.

The principal difference between bargaining and persuasion through rewards is that in bargaining the rewards are not initiated at the outset by management. Instead, they are management's response to proposals made by the employees themselves. Bargaining, therefore, is related also to the processes of discussion and participation, which we shall discuss later in this chapter.

The essence of bargaining is compromise. To maximize the achievement of their goals and the satisfaction of their needs, both management and those affected by a change must give way on some of the points on which they would have liked to secure agreement.

Often, a change will bring into focus those areas where management's interests are in conflict with those of the workers. Management can identify some of these areas before they actually change anything (see chapter 5). Other areas of conflict will become apparent when complaints and grievances are voiced after the change is announced. Sometimes, a grievance will identify directly the area of conflict. In other cases, the complaint will be merely a symptom of the conflict.

Management must give careful and open-minded consideration to all complaints and grievances. In doing so, they must recognize that the workers' and the union's points of view towards the change are often distinctly different from their own. Typically, this difference is based on the fact that management and the workers tend to assign unlike priorities to their values.

Once the complaints and grievances are known, and the areas of conflict of interest are identified, management can then consider the possibilities of making concessions or compromises. In cases where those affected by a change are likely to sustain economic, personal or social losses that are both real and unavoidable, management should consider concessions or compromises seriously. The relative costs of such concessions or compromises must be evaluated. These costs must be compared not only with those of alternative courses of action, but also with the costs that might be incurred if the change were not successful. In such comparisons of costs, management should estimate the total effect of both making and not making the compromise. They must consider not only what would be the direct financial effects, but also the influence on such factors as precedent, employee morale, quality of product and public relations. Often, the cost of compromise will be more than offset by the increased probability that the change will yield the anticipated benefits.

Bargaining is most feasible and useful when there is a union representing the employees. With a union, there is an established mechanism for bargaining. Also, bargaining is recognized and accepted by both management and the union as the normal method for reaching agreement.

For bargaining with a union to be successful, management must be aware of and willing to consider the union's institutional needs for involvement in all matters concerning its members' welfare (see p. 45). Management must be willing to inform the union well in advance of any impending changes. They must also be willing to listen to the union's objections.

But if the union's objections consistently prove to be fruitless, the mere gestures of notification and listening are not enough for management to gain the union's support of a proposed change. The union must perceive management as willing to make concessions and accept suggestions. Management should begin bargaining only with the following premise: that it may be necessary to accept certain suggestions and make certain compromises that are not entirely desirable from management's viewpoint, because a reasonably adequate solution supported by the union is better than an ideal solution opposed by the union.

Bargaining with non-union groups may be more difficult, because the process itself has not become formalized. Nevertheless, management might deal with informal leaders or with committees selected by the employees themselves. For bargaining to be successfulful in this context, our above-listed principles of early notification, open-minded consideration and willingness to compromise should also apply. In addition, the participants in any bargaining discussions must feel free to express their opinions and objections openly. They must have confidence and trust in the fairness of their management because they have no union whose power can protect their interests.

The techniques of persuading employees to accept a change

depend on the offer of rewards. This can be done either unilaterally or within the framework of bargaining. The success of this approach depends on how effectively management:

* *Match the rewards they offer to their employees' needs and goals.*

* *Give serious consideration to all complaints and suggestions.*

* *Give some concessions in order to achieve the major portion of their objectives.*

Security and Guarantees

The most efficient means for management to minimize feelings of insecurity, and particularly fears of redundancy, is to guarantee that these fears are groundless. A pledge that there will be no redundancy as a consequence of a specific change can often make possible its genuine acceptance.

Implementing such a pledge can be a challenging task for management. Essentially, they can achieve no redundancy in a changing situation in but six ways:

* Not replacing by engagement from outside the company those who leave the organization in the natural course of events (e.g. those who retire, die, resign voluntarily, and those who are sacked).

* Reabsorbing work being done by subcontractors and employing those who are surplus on that work.

* Retraining the redundant employees and transferring or upgrading them to other work.

* Reducing or eliminating overtime working.

* Handling any additional work from expansion of business with no additionally engaged labour until all those who are surplus have been productively re-employed.

* Inventing and implementing new areas of business activity.

Fulfilling a pledge of no redundancy can be both difficult and expensive. Management may have to spend some of the savings from the change. Also, they may have to wait longer for these savings to be realized. Nevertheless, the cost of guaranteeing the workers' security must be compared with the costs of their resisting the change. As we have already noted in our prior discussion of rewards, in most instances management will probably discover that to provide such guarantees makes sound economic sense.

There is no alternative so effective as a guarantee of no redundancy for eliminating fears of insecurity. It is conceivable, however, that a management might be unable to apply the above methods for solving the problem of a surplus of labour from a change.

In such circumstances, management might consider another approach. This is based on a guarantee of continued income for each surplus employee until he is working in another comparable job, either within or outside the company. In this approach, management would undertake to help each surplus individual find another suitable job. Until this occurs, the employee's income would continue to be maintained by the company as a supplement to any unemployment benefits from the state.

We believe, however, that such an approach is a poor second best to a guarantee of no redundancy. Although the employee might feel secure about the continuity of his income, he would nevertheless feel uneasy about the impending changes in his personal life. He would undoubtedly have many unanswered questions and apprehensions about his new job and new environment. Because of these questions and fears, he might still resist the change, although perhaps in a slightly less intense manner than if he were to be made redundant with no guarantees of any kind.

The following is an example of how a declining industry handled the unavoidable threat to the security of the employees involved:

> A notable example of how to avoid industrial strife is the old tinplate industry of Wales. Here the employers realized soon after the war that there would be a decline in the industry. They went to the unions and predicted the closure of many of the small tinplate handmills and that unless something could be done this would cause redundancy and hardship in a few years. As a result of these talks, beginning in 1946, there was time to do something about the situation and to find alternative employment for the men. It was also agreed to set up a fund, so that by the time of the final closures in 1958 there was almost £1 m. available to compensate the men who became redundant. Throughout this decline there were few restrictive practices.[1]

[1] 'Eye on restrictive practices—3', *The Times*, London, 19.2.65, p. 7.

An individual's feelings of insecurity can also be heightened if he fears that he might be unable to perform adequately in the new situation. Management can do much to reduce this fear by providing training. A carefully designed programme of training can often help to make a change successful.

For such a training programme to be effective, it must be designed to help people discard those attitudes and working habits that might impede their ability to perform well in the new situation. Only after this has been accomplished can new knowledge and skills be developed. There must be a period of unlearning before any new learning can take place.

There is another way in which management can benefit from a training programme. The very act of establishing one provides evidence that management are doing everything possible to help those involved cope with the change. Such a reassuring demonstration of management's support should reduce the feelings of insecurity so often associated with feelings of inadequacy.

Finally, to lessen any feelings of insecurity from factors other than fears of redundancy or inadequacy, management can use the technique of discussion. Through discussion, there can be developed a realistic understanding of the change and its probable consequences. Such understanding can do much to dispel those fears resulting from misunderstanding or lack of information. We shall examine the technique of discussion in the following section.

The strongest cause of feelings of insecurity, fears of redundancy, can best be minimized by management's pledge that no redundancy will result from the change. As a less desirable alternative, management might promise to maintain the incomes of those who become surplus until they find other work. To reduce feelings of insecurity resulting from fears of inadequacy, management can offer training programmes tailored to employees' needs. Management can deal with the remaining reasons for insecure feelings by developing an understanding of what are likely to be the consequences of the change.

Understanding and Discussion

Earlier, we suggested that when as many as possible of those people involved in a change understand as much as possible about it and its consequences, their resistance is likely to be reduced. It is up to management to develop this understanding.

> Resistance will be prevented to the degree that the changer helps the changees to develop their own understanding of the need for the change, and an explicit awareness of how they feel about it, and what can be done about their feelings.[1]

Such understanding can be based only on sufficient information that is both factual and accurate. Management can transmit information about a proposed change and its probable consequences to those affected or concerned in a variety of ways. Fundamentally, there are only two possible approaches to communication: written and oral. Below is a list of the variety of media that can be employed:

Written media

- Notices on bulletin boards
- Brief, scheduled newsletters specially composed and individually addressed
- Articles in the company newspaper or magazine
- Special memoranda delivered to each individual either at work or at his home
- News releases for general publication in community newspapers
- Posters and signs
- Specially designed and constructed visual displays such as models, mock-ups, etc.
- Films, filmstrips and other audio-visual presentations
- Self-administered programmed instruction

Oral media

- Formal orientation, indoctrination and training meetings
- Announcements and messages on company public-address systems
- Group discussions (face-to-face)
- Individual discussions (face-to-face)

All of these media can be used to transmit information. Each can be employed with effectiveness. No single means, however, should be relied upon exclusively. The more complex the change, the greater should be the variety of media employed. When many are used, the possibilities are increased that everyone involved is being reached with a maximum of information.

[1] A. Zander, 'Resistance to change—its analysis and prevention', *Advanced Management*, **XV**, No. 1, January 1950, p. 9.

All but two of these approaches, however, have severe limitations. The mere transmission of information is no assurance that people will gain understanding. Several conditions are required for the development of understanding in a changing situation:

* Information must be readily accessible, factual and accurate.

* Information must be communicated in language or in a form that is readily understandable.

* Information must answer the questions that are being asked . . . not only what is to happen, but also how, why, when, where and to whom.

* There must be a way to confirm that real understanding has been achieved.

All of the above media can fulfil the first two conditions. But the only means of communication that can achieve all four conditions are those that depend on face-to-face discussions conducted in an atmosphere of free interchange of ideas. In such discussions, the employees can ask questions directly of the manager. Furthermore, a sensitive and observant manager can learn a great deal about the employees' unexpressed fears from the nature of their questions and from the manner in which they are asked. Also, the manager himself can raise questions to test the accuracy of his predictions of reactions to the change and confirm the existence of these fears. He can then reduce these fears by supplying additional information. He can also estimate how widely particular questions or fears are shared within the group. Finally, the manager can ask questions to help him evaluate how much understanding has been developed. Only in the give-and-take exchanges that are possible in a discussion can the manager be certain that the needed information is being supplied and that understanding is genuinely being achieved.

In addition, through discussion, an individual who may previously have built up feelings of irritation and anger from the frustrations of the change can find a ready outlet to release his hostile feelings. He can 'blow off steam' by voicing his fears and by giving vent to his feelings in words. Such a release or 'catharsis' can in itself be a valuable by-product of discussions. Through the safety-valve of discussion, aggressive feelings that might otherwise have been expressed in restriction of output, in 'mistakes', or in sabotage can be released with little harmful effect.

It matters little whether a discussion is carried on in a formal and structured manner (e.g. orientation and training meetings and conferences), or on an informal and unstructured basis. What does matter, however, is that a proper atmosphere be established by the manager. He must help the participants to develop the feeling that they are free to raise any questions or to make any comments they wish, without fear of reprisal.

The manager can do this first by encouraging individuals to raise questions and to explain their meaning. Also, he must respond freely and openly with honest answers. He must distinguish between facts, opinions and speculation. He must take care not to appear to judge the questioner for voicing fears or queries that seem ridiculous or suspect in their motivation. Finally, he must allow sufficient time for the discussion to develop, and for as many that so desire to speak.

At first, a manager's success in establishing this kind of an atmosphere in his discussions will depend almost entirely on the nature of his past relationships with the participants. However, if he persists and is consistent in this approach over a long enough period of time, and if the participants learn that they can in fact speak up with no distasteful consequences, a manager can to some extent overcome a past history of mistrust and suspicion.

Whatever medium of communication is used, the language must be readily understandable. The problem of language often arises when a change is being explained by a staff specialist. Staff specialists often believe that the reasons for a change are so complicated and specialized that it is impossible to explain them to operating people, whether they be supervisors or workers. True, operating personnel probably would find it difficult to understand some of the analytical techniques used by staff specialists. If, however, a specialist makes no effort to translate his ideas into language that can be understood by supervisors and operatives, they may soon conclude that the specialist is either confusing or misleading them with his technical jargon and complicated formulae and figures. Such a reaction can be harmful to the successful implementation of the change.

> A staff specialist was temporarily successful in 'selling' a change based on a complicated mathematical formula to a foreman who really did not understand it. The whole thing

backfired, however, when the foreman tried to sell it to his operating people. They asked him a couple of sharp questions that he could not answer. His embarrassment about this led him to resent and resist the change so much that eventually the whole proposition fell through. This was unfortunate in terms not only of human relations but also of technological progress in the plant.[1]

Clearly, it is not necessary for operating personnel to understand the reasons for a change in the same terms or to the same extent of detail as does the staff specialist. They must, however, be able to visualize the proposed change and its reasons in terms of their own experiences on the job. Any inability on their part to understand the basis for the change and the change itself reflects a failure by both management and staff specialists to provide adequate explanations.

A lack of understanding can result in heightened anxiety about the possible consequences of a change. This, in turn, can result in resistant behaviour. In addition, it is likely that because of this lack those performing the work will derive less satisfaction from their jobs. This should be of concern to management, particularly during a change. When an individual does not understand what he is doing, he cannot exercise those abilities of which he, as a human being, is uniquely capable. These abilities are the application of informed and intelligent judgments to the performance of his work. When anyone is deprived of the opportunity to make meaningful judgments, he can become increasingly frustrated. Not only will both he and his work suffer, but so also will the company.

During a change, the operation of many of the normal mechanisms and channels of communication are often disrupted and impaired. To compensate for this, management must devote special attention and make an extra effort to communicate a full understanding of every aspect of the change and its probable consequences. They should use every practicable technique of communication. The language used must be related to the frame of reference of those to whom the communications are addressed. Of all the possible communication techniques, management should make the greatest use of face-to-face discussions, both with individuals and with groups. This technique is the most effective method

[1] P. R. Lawrence, 'How to deal with resistance to change', *The Harvard Business Review*, **32**, No. 3, May–June 1954.

for ensuring that answers are being given to those questions of genuine concern to the people involved. Also, discussions are the most effective means for determining how much true understanding is being achieved.

Time and Timing

Previously, we noted that when management are willing to discuss openly with their employees all aspects of an impending change, it is desirable that ample time be planned between the initial mention of the change and its actual initiation. Management should use this interval to ensure that all involved attain a maximum of understanding of the change and its probable consequences.

Management should plan the length of this interval by working out a balance between two considerations. Often these will be in conflict with one another. The first of these is concerned with the question of how long it is necessary for the processes of accommodation and rationalization to take place for most of the people involved. The second consideration is an evaluation of those elements in the situation which determine when the change must be instituted and implemented and when the benefits must be realized.

Management should first question and re-examine the reasons and premises on which they based their original timing. Must the change actually be competed by date X? How much of it must really be completed by date X? What would be the consequences of postponing the completion of the change to dates Y or Z?

To achieve a balance between these two considerations, management should evaluate the relative costs of two alternatives: (a) delaying the introduction of the change and the realization of optimum benefits; and (b) increasing the risk of resistance, with the resultant probability of reduced benefits. In many instances, management may discover that it will be economic to delay the change until its acceptance is ensured. If management decide not to delay, resistance may cause not only a reduction in the possible benefits but also probable delays in their realization. As for the date of completion of the change, therefore, it might not matter which of the above approaches management chooses. The resultant benefits, however, might be very different. It might prove worthwhile, therefore, for management to devote sufficient time during the early phases of the change so that accommodation and rationalization can occur and so that understanding can be developed.

When management are establishing the timing for a change, they should also consider the relationship of that change to other events both in the company and in the community. Several questions should be answered. First, is the change being timed so as to coincide with any other events that may jeopardize its successful implementation? Let us consider two examples:

* It is planned to automate a manufacturing operation in one department, while in another department the workforce is being reduced as a consequence of a drop in consumer demand for the company's products. Because of the resultant redundancies, the entire workforce is likely to become increasingly aware and fearful of losing their jobs. This is hardly an opportune time for introducing a new process that could result in further redundancies.

* In a community of moderate size, Company A has introduced a computer into its office. Because of inept planning and poor management, this change was handled badly. The employees' reaction to the change was unfavourable, and the company received some poor publicity in the local press. Company B in this same community is also about to introduce a computer into its office. Its management decide to delay the introduction for several months and to devote the time gained to improving their plans for the change and to increasing the extent of discussions with the employees to be affected.

Another question that should be examined is whether or not the contemplated change could be so timed as to coincide with other events that might improve the chances for its successful implementation. For example:

> The Acme Products Company has completed a major study of its distribution operations. If certain improvements are made in the methods of operation, the company will be able to distribute its products with about 800 fewer employees. The company at present subcontracts many of its distribution operations. From the study, it appears economic for the Acme Company to handle directly about 75% of its total distribution activities. The contracts with most of the subcontracting firms are scheduled for renegotiation in 12 months. Management decide to time the improvements in distribution opera-

tions to coincide with the break-points in these contracts. Thus, most of the employees who would otherwise have been redundant can be retained by the reabsorbtion of the work currently subcontracted.

Finally, consideration should be given to the question of whether or not the change is timed most opportunely from the standpoint of management's bargaining position. For example:

> In a peak period of production, a 'bottleneck' develops in one manufacturing operation involving a small group of highly skilled men. After studying this operation, management conclude that it can be streamlined and improved to the extent that the existing workforce should be able to cope successfully with the greatly increased but temporary flow of work. This, however, will require the men's cooperation. After further analyses of the situation, management decide to postpone introducing the changes until after the production peak has subsided. They can deal with the immediate crisis by subcontracting some of the work. This decision is made because management realize that while the bottleneck exists the skilled operatives are in a particularly strong bargaining position. Their morale cannot be permitted to deteriorate because productivity cannot be impaired. Also, they are likely to be fearful that some of their number might become redundant when their workload decreases after the peak of activity has subsided to a more 'normal' level.
> These fears could be handled more effectively later on when the problem of redundancy is immediate and definite, instead of when it is still somewhat vague and in the future.

Management should time a change on the basis of several carefully considered factors. In so doing, they must compare the costs of alternative courses of action. In most cases, they should discover that the cost of devoting more time to preparing their employees for the change will be less than the cost of increased resistance and decreased benefits. Also, management should time the change so that it is coordinated with other events of significance occurring both within and outside the company.

Involvement and Participation

We have already noted that personal involvement in making some of the decisions about a change often has several beneficial effects.

The personal satisfactions derived from the job are increased. The commitment to carry out these decisions is intensified. Resistance is decreased. Also, we have just considered how face-to-face discussions can help to develop an understanding of a change and its probable consequences. The process of participation is a method of managing based on both discussion and involvement.

The objective of a participative approach is to achieve acceptance by a group of people that they are taking part in planning, initiating and implementing a change rather than being the recipients of its effects. The participative approach is most likely to be effective when it is applied to relatively small groups, and when it concerns changes that are essentially local in nature.

A manager can use the participative method in a variety of ways. These can vary according to how much personal involvement in decision-making the manager wishes to achieve or permit. The extent of personal involvement can range from discussing problems and voicing opinions and feelings to actually making and implementing decisions.

At its most superficial level, participation can be achieved through individual or group consultation. This process is but a slight extension of the face-to-face discussions that we have already described. In a discussion, the manager typically describes his proposals and intentions. He then invites those present to voice their comments and feelings. In the process of consultation, the manager carries this approach a step further. He asks those present to make suggestions about how the change might best be accomplished.

In consultation, there is an implicit understanding that management are under no obligation to accept any of the ideas offered, so long as they are given serious consideration. If, however, over a period of time all suggestions are rejected, the employees will come to regard consultation as a pretence and a fraud. If this attitude should develop, a manager's relationship with his subordinates can be severely damaged.

In consultation, many valuable ideas often come to light. The man actually doing the job on a day-to-day basis is usually more knowledgeable about it than anyone else.

> Management in a small steel plant was facing an unusually stubborn problem. Product quality had fallen off and none of the engineering staff was able to come up with a solution. Expensive consultants also failed to stem the increasing flow

> of scrap. Finally, the plant manager called some of the old-timers together, explained the problem, and told them the firm would face bankruptcy if the problem wasn't solved. After a few minutes' discussion, one of these workers suggested the cause of the trouble and how to solve it. When asked why he hadn't produced this important information before, he answered, 'I wasn't asked'.[1]

Any employee can take pride in and derive satisfaction from knowing that his suggestion is being considered. These feelings are intensified if the suggestion is actually adopted. But if the suggestion is rejected, then he must be made to understand why. If the manager is effective in his explanations, consultation can still be productive. There are three reasons for this. First, the very fact that the employee had an opportunity both to express himself and to be given serious attention can be, in itself, beneficial to his attitude and morale. Also, by understanding why his suggestion was not acceptable, the employee may reach a better understanding of the change. Finally, he may be encouraged to offer better suggestions in the future.

The following is an example of consultation as applied to a large group through the medium of written communication:

> The Arcturus Products Company employs about 3500 employees in research, development and the manufacture of a complex series of consumer products. All personnel policies and procedures were evolved through a system of consultation with all members of management and supervision, and with a representative Employees' Committee. Suggestions for new policies or modifications to the existing policies and procedures are submitted to a Personnel Policy Committee made up of members of top management. When so ordered by this comittee, a *First Draft* of a proposed new policy (or modification to an existing policy) is issued on yellow paper. This is circulated to about 300 members of management and to the members of the Employees' Committee. These individuals are invited to discuss the proposed change with as many other employees as possible, and to return their written comments to the Personnel Policy Committee. If there is no adverse reaction of significance, the policy is then re-issued as a formal

[1] G. Strauss and L. Sayles, *Personnel, The Human Problems of Management*, Prentice-Hall, Englewood Cliffs, New Jersey, 1960, p. 150.

> *Instruction* on white paper, to be included in the Personnel Policy Manuals that are maintained in each department.
>
> If, on the other hand, there is a significant response to the *First Draft*, the comments are evaluated in terms both of their content and frequency of occurrence. A *Second Draft* (also on yellow paper) of the proposed policy is then issued to the same group. This is a modification of the *First Draft*, with the changes reflecting the comments. Again, comments are requested on the *Seond Draft* and the process described above continues until a formal *Instruction* is issued. Occasionally, when the responses are strongly negative, the proposed change in policy (or new policy) may be dropped altogether. Sometimes a proposal will be reissued in as many as four separate and different drafts before it is finally accepted as a formal policy. This process has the disadvantage of taking a long time between the introduction of a new proposal for a change and its formal institution as a policy. On the other hand, this disadvantage is offset by the fact that all changes in personnel policy are introduced smoothly. By the time they become official practice, these changes are well understood and accepted, not only by all levels of management, but also by the employees as well. This is because the change has been thoroughly discussed, and is familiar to all.

If it is to operate at a deeper level, the participative process should include some involvement in actual decision-making. Not only should the manager elicit suggestions from those involved in the change, but he should also encourage them to share, to an extent, in making the decisions related to that change. This method of managing has received considerable attention in recent years. A fundamental research study in the participative process involved a pyjama factory in the United States.[1]

> In this pyjama factory, there were constant changes in the style of the product and in the methods of production. These changes were often opposed strongly by the female workers. Opposition was expressed in several forms. For instance, when employees were transferred from one job to another, they often took a longer time to learn the new job than did those entirely new to the company. Also, 62% of the transferred employees

[1] L. Coch and J. R. P. French, 'Overcoming resistance to change', *Human Relations*, **1**, No. 4 (1948), p. 12.

either failed to achieve a satisfactory level of production or else quit altogether. Some of the groups restricted their output and engaged in aggressive behaviour against management. This resistance was caused by frustration over loss of status, the difficulties in learning new methods, and the fear of not being able to regain their earlier levels of proficiency. Economic fears were less significant, because the girls received a liberal learning allowance during the period of adjustment to make up for any losses in piecework earnings.

As an experiment, four groups were established. Each was subjected to changes in their methods of work. These changes affected less than 10% of their total work. For each of these four groups, a different method was used to introduce the change. The results were carefully recorded to determine what, if any, resistance occurred.

The *control group* followed the traditional routines for instituting changes. They were gathered together and told in general terms that the new method was made necessary because of competition in the pyjama business. The new piecework pay rate was announced, and the members of the group were given an opportunity to ask questions.

The *partial-participation* group attended a meeting at which the need for change was explained in a dramatic manner. Management emphasized that as a consequence of the change, the company could produce pyjamas more competitively and gain a greater share of the market. As a result of this, the employees would enjoy better working conditions and have greater job security. The members of this group agreed in principle to the change. They elected a committee to assist management in developing the necessary plans and in establishing the new piecework pay rates.

Two *total-participation groups* were formed, each smaller than the partial-participation group. These groups followed a procedure similar to the partial-participation group, except that all of the operatives participated in planning how the change was to take place. The groups discussed how existing work methods could be improved. When the new methods were agreed, all were trained and then observed by the time-study men so that the new piecework pay rates could be established.

The most striking difference in the resultant behaviour was between the control group and the two total-participation groups. The output of the control group dropped immediately to about two-thirds its previous level. Production remained at this lower rate throughout the period of 30 days after the change had been introduced. The researchers reported that, 'Resistance developed almost immediately after the change occurred. Marked expressions of aggression against management occurred, such as conflict with the methods engineer . . . hostility towards the supervisor, deliberate restriction of production and lack of cooperation with the supervisor. There were 17% quits in the first 40 days. Grievances were filed about piece-rates; but when the rate was checked, it was found to be a little "loose".'

In contrast with the control group, the total-participation groups (and almost to the same extent the partial-participation group) were very cooperative. After a small initial drop in their output, they soon achieved a production level 40% higher than that of the control group. There were no signs of aggressive behaviour towards management and there were no quits during the experimental period.

From this study, the researchers concluded that when people affected by a change became involved in making the decisions which determined how it was to be implemented, they tended not to resist it. This conclusion, however, is valid only in certain instances. The problem of how a manager can achieve genuine participation in a changing situation is more complex than one might realize from this research.

In a more recent study, C. Argyris[1] found that the 30 employees affected were apparently unconcerned with their management's failure to use participation with them in implementing a change.

Management decided to mechanize production to cut costs and prices. No opportunity was given to the employees affected to become involved in planning this change. Management simply made an announcement of the change beforehand. There were no other communications until the process was ready for installation. Then, the men were shown the new process, briefed about it, and given a demonstration. The new process required little skill and meant that there would be a

[1] C. Argyris, in *Modern Organization Theory* (ed. M. Haire), Wiley, New York, 1959, p. 148.

> significant reduction in the skill required of the men to do the work.
>
> Through interviews, it was determined that in the culture of that organization the men's most important needs were for job security, for fair wages, for control over their immediate work environment and for comfortable social relationships. They apparently had no interest in becoming involved in the organization's activities, except for their own immediate jobs. Management purposely set loose piece-rates so that wage levels were maintained. With the change, job insecurity was increased somewhat because of increased dependency on the success of the particular product (and on the Sales Department). Nevertheless, 83% of those affected stated that, 'they did not care that they were not included in the planning of the changes. That is management's worry'. Ninety-two per cent viewed the changes as necessary if the company were to remain competitive. Although there was concern over possible reductions in quality, there was no apparent concern about the de-skilling of the jobs.
>
> A typical comment by one of the men was, 'I think management introduced the merry-go-round (nickname for the new process) correctly. There's no need in calling the people in and wasting a hell of a lot of time. You tell them what you plan to do, you guarantee their job security, and then let them think about it. When you're ready, you put it in. Sure they complain a little bit, but it's quieted down now.'

The concept of 'using participation' has become quite loosely understood and rather fashionable in some management circles. Many managers now think of it as a 'good thing' in the same way that they regard other techniques currently in vogue, such as elaborate programmes of management development.

In actuality, participation means different things to different managers. To some, it is a device for 'masterminding' and manipulating people to share a viewpoint already held by the manager. To others, it is merely a ritual to be observed so that there will be an illusion created that the employees have some voice in what is happening to them. Such views differ widely from the true meaning of participation.

> Participation does not mean winning friends and influencing people. Rather, it is analogous to the good salesman's sincere

concern for the potential customer. Even more basically, it is a means for the company to exercise its reponsibility to the people who work there—to provide its people with a sense of belonging based on human dignity.[1]

Participation can be applied to a broad range of problems. Let us consider several examples:[2]

* A company planning an expansion invited help from the foreman group in deciding where to locate the new plant and which foremen to transfer to it. The foremen joined in a study of alternatives, recommended a new location and drew up a list of their number to be assigned there. At that point the layout of the plant came up for discussion. The participation of the employees of the department which was to be expanded into the new plant was requested. The group pored over drawings, made three-dimensional models, and recommended changes in facilities, equipment, layout, parking areas, services and other matters that reduced the bill for the new plant considerably.

* A company wanted to introduce a rating and evaluation programme for middle-management people as a part of its executive development programme. Rating systems from consultants were available, but the problem was turned over to the group to be rated and the members developed their own system, which was more stringent than any proposed by outside firms.

* Another company, in the sales field, put the problem of territory boundaries, quotas and commissions before a representation of its sales force. This group made recommendations to management which showed real insight into the problem and also an understanding of its intricate detail. The group also suggested that it administer and review the matter at regular intervals.

* In the office, groups have reviewed records, reports, forms, methods, procedures and equipment; hundreds of examples of improvement in paper work through participation are known. For example, one office group found a lengthy report that had been compiled by it for some time and distributed monthly in a

[1] L. B. Moore, 'Too much management, too little change', *Harvard Business Review*, **34**, No. 1, January–February 1956, p. 41.

[2] *Ibid.*

large quantity, but which was no longer used or needed in the company. It was quickly eliminated and the girls released to more meaningful activity.

True participation cannot be created simply by management decree. It is not possible to appoint managers or staff specialists with an inherent ability to 'get participation'. Even if a well-meaning manager ordered his supervisors to 'get back to your sections and start participation', the result would probably be quite remote from the genuine involvement of employees in making decisions.

Real participation depends on the feelings and attitudes of the people involved. The mechanistic act of assembling a group for discussions is insufficient motivation for participation to be generated. What, then, are the prerequisite conditions necessary for true participation to take place? (The following discussion can be applied to unions as well as to groups of or individual employees.)

A basic requirement for participation is that the employees involved *want* to participate. In the cultural beliefs and norms of the organization (and to some extent of the society as a whole), there must be some need for involvement in the way the work is planned and organized. As we have already seen from the Argyris study (pp. 106–107), when this need is absent or subordinated to other more pressing needs there would be few benefits, and possibly even some disadvantages, to be gained from attempting to achieve participation.

It is quite possible, however, that an apparent lack of concern for involvement is a defensive rationalization developed by the employees because they realize that management are not genuinely interested in real participation. Instead, they believe that management want to use participation as a manipulative device to 'mastermind' them into accepting a change about which they are doubtful or fearful.

Fundamentally, the employees asked to participate must believe that their manager or supervisor is sincere and honest in his intention. Furthermore, they must believe that, if their ideas have merit, there will be a reasonable possibility of their adoption and implementation. For these beliefs to exist, there must first be a relationship between manager and worker based on mutual respect, confidence and trust. If these elements are not present, then any attempts to generate participation would be regarded with suspicion and mistrust. The true motives behind any attempts to use participation for 'masterminding' would soon be perceived. This would result in a further deterioration of the relations between the manager and his subordinates.

There is another prerequisite condition for successful participation. The manager or supervisor must feel secure in his position and role. Some managers may be reluctant to attempt the development of participation with their subordinates because of certain preconceptions about their managerial role. For instance, a manager might believe that to ask for advice or opinions from his subordinates would be a sign of weakness. He might believe that if he invited participation he would be revealing to his subordinates that he was not omniscient or omnipotent. Thus, he might feel that any involvement of his subordinates in making decisions that were his perogative alone would endanger his status as a manager. Anyone with these beliefs would be surprised to learn that when employees are permitted and encouraged by their manager to participate, their esteem for him often tends to increase rather than to decrease.

If a manager can bring himself to risk his status in the eyes of his subordinates by involving them in some form of participation, he may be amazed at the consequences:

> The manager who wishes to get participation started should logically begin with a situation that is not too complex, political or emotional. If possible, it should be obvious, both to him and to the group members, that he could benefit from the advice of those around him. A slow, easy start is better than a sensational beginning, for this is a great change.
> He may come out in the open and state the change and ask the group to help, on the basis that confession is good for the soul and prompts sympathetic cooperation; or he may want to get his feet a bit wet before committing himself to the change since, being human, he like everyone else resists being pushed into the new. In the latter case he might start asking people for ideas and then listen them out. This technique is perfect for breaking up yes-man conferences and developing constructive ideas. Here is the kind of thing that happens:
>
> A plant superintendent who had become conscious of his tendency to run the meeting decided to change his tactics; he would ask for ideas and suggestions and then shut up. After a painful silence during which time the yes-men were moving

> their heads the other way looking for someone to speak up, two supposed incompetents quietly but definitely took a long-standing situation apart, called a spade a spade, and laid out a possible solution as neatly as a trained surgeon performs an appendectomy. The superintendent listened goggle-eyed and amazed.[1]

A third prerequisite condition for participation is absence of commitment on the manager's part to any one course of action. He must be open-minded to the possibilities for alternative approaches. When others are invited to participate in making decisions, some of their suggestions will probably not only be different from those of the manager but will also be as valid. Some of these ideas may even be superior. If the manager is convinced from the outset that his method is the best and only means of accomplishing the change, then he would be wise not even to attempt the involvement of others in a participative effort. Any such attempt would soon be perceived as meaningless and essentially dishonest.

Ideally, a manager should consider the objectives of the change to be of primary importance. Whatever method he uses to accomplish these objectives should be of secondary importance (see chapter 1). If these are the manager's priorities, there should be ample latitude for the adoption and use of any worthwhile ideas generated through participation.

However, even when a manager is committed to a particular method of approach, there will inevitably be some elements of the change that can be accomplished in a variety of ways, any one of which would be acceptable. He might select one or more of these elements as the subject for participative decision-making. In this way, he can control the areas of participation and yet gain some degree of personal involvement among those affected by the change. For example:

* A manager is moving his manufacturing department to a new location. This move involves a number of changes in the location and interrelationships of the individual operations, as well as changes in the methods of handling the materials. These changes have been predetermined by industrial engineers. The manager agrees fully with these changes, and is convinced there

[1] L. B. Moore, 'Too much management, too little change', *Harvard Business Review*, **34**, No. 1, January–February 1956, p. 41.

will be significant reductions in operating costs. Nevertheless, the manager is quite open-minded about other elements of these changes: the placement, design and decor of the employees' lounges and other facilities; the decor of the entire department; and some details of the specific arrangements of individual work stations. The manager designates these areas as problems for his employees to solve. Because the manager allows them to decide some elements of the change, the employees become personally involved in the change as a whole. As a result, they are cooperative about many aspects of the change that they might otherwise have resisted.

* A manager decides that his secretary should have a new and better typewriter. He defines the objectives of this change to his secretary (e.g. performance, cost, typeface), and then suggests that she decide on the particular typewriter that she would like. Thus, the final decision to purchase will be a joint one.

Still another condition necessary for effective participation is the manager's willingness to give credit and recognition openly to all contributions of merit made by others to the realization of the change. Also, if impracticable ideas are offered, the manager must ensure that the contributors receive full explanations. Such explanations must be both understandable and acceptable.

By now it should be evident that a manager's attitudes, and particularly his feelings of self-confidence and personal security, are crucial to the achievement of successful participation. A manager must be able to admit to himself, as well as to others, the possibility that his subordinates (even if they are operatives) might have suggestions about the conduct of a change as valid as his own. Such an admission requires considerable self-assurance.

> The fact that participation is not used in our businesses rests with the managers on every level. I have long felt that they are deterred largely because of their preconceptions. The thought of the manager asking for advice goes against the administrative grain. As the boss, he thinks that he cannot show those under him that he does not know all the answers. He cannot ever let them take control away from him for he will lose his managerial position, or at least his status.[1]

[1] L. B. Moore, 'Too much management, too little change', *Harvard Business Review*, **34**, No. 1, January–February 1956, p. 41.

The last condition necessary for effective participation is the employees' willingness to voice their comments and to offer suggestions once they have been encouraged to do so. Participation will not work with people who are passive or apathetic. Such attitudes are usually a result of their responses either to the previous behaviour of management or to prevailing cultural beliefs and norms.

If *all* these conditions are not present in a changing situation, a manager should approach very cautiously the use of participation as a supervisory technique. If, on the other hand, all these conditions are satisfied, the use of participation in a changing situation can yield several significant benefits:

* Participation helps to develop a better and more complete understanding of the change, its causes and its probable consequences.

* Participation is a means of unfreezing fixed attitudes, stereotypes or cultural beliefs which are held either by management or by the workforce, and which conflict with the accomplishment of the change. Through participation, these beliefs can be re-examined in a more objective light. Thus, participation can help open up one's mind. An example occurred in the pyjama plant previously discussed.[1] During World War II, the company's staff psychologist attempted to persuade management (because of the shortage of manpower) to abandon their policy of not engaging workers over 30 years of age. Management immediately opposed this idea, insisting that older women required a long training period, were absent more, and never worked at top speed. When the psychologist referred to the good performance of those older women currently employed, management dismissed these examples as exceptional cases. Then the psychologist tried another approach. He involved management in a research project to determine how much money the company was losing by employing older women. Management themselves determined the criteria to be used and decided how the data were to be collected. Management became actively involved. To their surprise, the data showed that older women were better in every respect. Because of their findings, management changed their policy and urged other companies to follow suit.

[1] A. J. Marrow and J. R. P. French, 'Overcoming a stereotype', *Journal of Social Issues*, **1**, No. 3 (1945), p. 33.

* Participation helps increase employees' confidence in management's intentions and objectives.

* Often, as a consequence of participation, first-hand ideas are contributed that result in better methods of introducing and implementing the change.

* Through participation people involve themselves in the change and become more committed to the decisions in which they took part.

* Participation sometimes serves to prevent poorly-conceived changes from being made.

* Through participation, staff specialists tend to broaden their outlook.

* Through participation, subordinates' capabilities can be developed.

An especially effective use of participation is the involvement of those employees concerned in diagnosing the particular problems underlying the need for a change. Diagnosis can result from participation in gathering the relevant facts. Because these individuals participated in developing the data that later led them to identify the problem requiring solution, they would tend to support the change designed to solve that problem.

> A number of high-level supervisors in a utility industry came to feel that the workers had many negative attitudes about their jobs which were due to poor supervisory practices. Each supervisor, quite naturally, felt that other supervisors were at fault. Top management set up a number of study groups in which the supervisors first learned how they could diagnose the causes of these negative attitudes. Each supervisor then returned to his own work place and gathered facts that would be necessary for him to analyse the causes of negative attitudes he could spot among his workers. Later the supervisors came together to report their findings. At this meeting their enthusiasm for change in their own practices was high because they had participated in gathering the facts which best

described their problems. People will be more likely to act in terms of information they gather themselves than in terms of information gathered by others and delivered to them.[1]

Participation is one of the most potentially effective managerial techniques for transforming any possible resistance to a change into active support. It is, however, a technique that must be used carefully when certain prerequisite conditions can be met.

Criticism, Ceremony, and Building on the Past

In a changing situation, a manager should try to avoid any actions that would lead to those involved feeling criticized. At least two courses of action are possible. First, he can make positive and constructive use of the past in all his communications about the change. Second, he can make deliberate use of ceremony and ritual.

Anthropologists have long known that in order to work effectively with any group of people it is essential to learn their customs, ceremonies, symbols and their expected ways of doing things. Changes can be introduced far more easily when adjustments are made to the past. One way of making such adjustments is to retain in the changed situation certain elements of past rituals and symbols.

> The chief psychiatrist of Nigeria's most important mental hospital was describing the application of European and American psychotherapeutic techniques in the treatment of some of his patients who were still part of a tribal culture. At the conclusion of a successful course of treatment, the patient could not feel himself to be wholly cured until he had sacrificed a goat to appease the gods responsible for his mental illness. Such a sacrifice is retained by the hospital as an essential part of the individual's treatment.

Another way of adjusting to the past is to place past practices in proper perspective to the proposed change. The value of these traditional methods of doing things should be acknowledged. But their value should be related to the way in which they fulfilled the requirements of past situations and circumstances. It should be made clear that the reason why such traditional practices are no longer adequate and must therefore be changed is because the

[1] A. Zander, 'Resistance to change—its analysis and prevention', *Advanced Management*, **XV**, No. 1, January 1950, p. 9.

present or future situation and circumstances require that practices and methods be different. Everyone involved should understand that the traditional methods were appropriate in the past but are now no longer appropriate because conditions are no longer the same. The difference in conditions must be emphasized. Clearly, no individual or group can be held to blame for changes in conditions.

A smooth transition from an established state to a new one can be ensured by the deliberate use of ceremony. Through ceremony, one's loyalty can be focused on the organization as a whole rather than on any particular individual. Also, ceremony helps people think in terms that are broader than their own immediate personal needs and desires.

It is not by chance that ceremonies are an important element in the conduct of the affairs of such long-lived institutions as the Church, the State and Universities. In our personal lives, ceremonies are a means for marking such major changes as birth, completion of education, marriage and death. At these occasions, gathering together relatives and friends and giving gifts and flowers help symbolize friendship and the unity of families. When we become involved in the ritual of the ceremony, we are able to lessen some of our own fears and pains that result from moving from one stage of life to another. The heightened emotional atmosphere of such ceremonies helps us to prepare for significant changes in our relationships with others.

Furthermore, a ceremony can be regarded as a public statement that, although changes are taking place, the fundamental values remain constant. In England, a new sovereign is hailed with, 'The King is dead; long live the King'. In France, it is, 'Plus ça change, plus c'est la même chose'.

Let us consider an illustration of how both an adjustment to the past and ceremony were used in introducing a new supervisor into a large restaurant.[1]

> The old supervisor had developed warm relationships with her subordinates. Therefore, the restaurant manager feared that her departure might affect adversely the morale of the entire organization. He therefore made careful preparations for introducing her successor. First, he discussed the problem of a replacement with both the old supervisor and her assist-

[1] Condensed from W. F. Whyte, *Human Relations in the Restaurant Industry*, McGraw-Hill, New York (1948), p. 319.

ant, the chef. The chef proposed a candidate for the job. Although this candidate had to be rejected, the reasons were explained to the chef.

Finally, a new supervisor was selected. She was introduced to her subordinates at a general meeting. The manager announced that the old supervisor was leaving. He noted how much she meant to the restaurant, and how she would be missed. The old supervisor then spoke emotionally about her regret at leaving her associates. Next, she introduced the new supervisor. She voiced her warm approval of the new supervisor, and asked her employees to cooperate with the new woman in the same way they had worked with her. The new supervisor then promised to do her best to follow in her predecessor's footsteps.

During the next few days, the new supervisor accompanied the old one, acquainting herself with the individuals and with the old supervisor's routine and methods of dealing with people. On the old supervisor's final day at work, the kitchen staff gave her a farewell party.

The new supervisor planned to make certain changes in the operation. Nevertheless, she was careful during her first several weeks to follow the pattern of human relations that her predecessor had established. Soon she was fully accepted by the group. Only then did she begin to introduce changes.

Thus, both the meeting at which the new supervisor was introduced and the farewell party for the old supervisor served a ceremonial function. These gatherings helped to make the change an accepted fact. They also helped the new supervisor acquire some of the prestige held by her predecessor. In her care to learn the existing routines and the old supervisor's methods of dealing with people, the new supervisor made it clear that she was not rejecting past practices or suggesting any criticism of her predecessor.

A manager may be tempted to be impatient with past practices and traditions, and to be cynical about the use of ceremony. Yet, in his rejection of these, he is failing to avail himself of useful means of reducing resistance to a change.

Flexibility and the Tentative Approach

So that the people involved in a change can feel some control over what happens to them, it is often desirable to introduce the change first as a tentative, trial exercise. Such a trial can be set up on the basis either of a finite period of time or of a designated group of people. The particular basis chosen should depend on the particular circumstances.

There are several advantages to a tentative, trial approach:

* Those involved are able to test their reactions to the new situation before committing themseles irrevocably.

* Those involved are able to acquire more facts on which to base their attitudes and behaviour towards the change.

* Those involved with strong preconceptions are in a better position to regard the change with greater objectivity. Consequently, they could review their preconceptions and perhaps modify some of them.

* Those involved are less likely to regard the change as a threat.

* Management are better able to evaluate the method of change and make any necessary modifications before carrying it out more fully.

These advantages would accrue from gaining some limited experience of the change while it is still capable of being further revised or modified.

Introducing a change on a tentative trial basis tends to reduce its threat to those affected. Consequently, their resistance to the change in its final form should be lessened.

Summary: The Scanlon Plan

Rather than summarize in the conventional manner the supervisory techniques discussed in this chapter, we shall take a different approach. It should be instructive to examine an unusual programme that makes use of many of these techniques, and that has produced some rather spectacular results for those managements with the courage, wisdom and opportunities to adopt this approach. This programme, designed to improve the operating effectiveness of an entire organization, is known as the Scanlon

Plan.[1] It has been gaining acceptance gradually in the past decade.[2]

The Scanlon plan has been known primarily as a kind of a group incentive plan, based on the sharing of profits. However, its scope and implications have considerably greater breadth. The profit-sharing aspects of the Scanlon plan are merely the means to an end: that of transforming both the attitude and the capability of the entire organization towards carrying out changes for improvement. The Scanlon plan has resulted in dramatic improvements in labour–management relations, developing organizational team-work, human motivation, and creating an environment where changes are accepted and supported rather than resisted. It is in this last context that we shall discuss this plan.

Briefly, the Scanlon plan consists of two basic elements: a wage formula which provides a group incentive; and a means for ensuring that all employees have an opportunity to participate in improving the effectiveness of the operation.

The objective of the wage formula is to permit all employees to share the rewards of increased productivity. Because each company develops its own formula, there is no 'standard' approach. Typically, however, the wage formula provides that every employee of the organization (often including the managing director) receives a monthly bonus. This is based on the monthly improvement in operating effectiveness. This improvement is usually measured in terms of the ratio of total payroll costs to the sales value of whatever is produced. The ratio and specific wage formula for each plant is developed through union–management negotiations. The monthly bonus is not only an incentive for better operating effect-

[1] This plan is named for the man who devised it, the late Joseph Scanlon, who rose from a rank-and-file worker in a steel plant in the United States to become the Research and Engineering Director of the steelworkers' union (United Steelworkers of America). Later, he became a lecturer at the Massachusetts Institute of Technology. For a more complete discussion of this plan, see: R. W. Davenport, 'Enterprise for everyone', *Fortune*, **41**, No. 1, January 1950, p. 55; W. F. Whyte *et al.*, 'The Scanlon plan', *Money and Motivation*, Harper, New York (1955), chapter 14; F. G. Lesieur (ed.), *The Scanlon Plan: A Frontier in Labor–Management Cooperation*, Wiley, New York: The Technology Press, Cambridge, 1958; G. Strauss and L. R. Sayles, 'The Scanlon plan: some organisational problems, *Human organisation*, **16**, No. 3, Fall 1957, p. 15.

[2] To date, the Scanlon plan has achieved limited acceptance. It is in operation in fewer than 50 companies in the United States. One of the most recent installations of this plan has been at the Linwood plant of the Pressed Steel Company (Great Britain) near Glasgow, Scotland. Early achievements at Linwood were reported in an article in *The Financial Times*, London, 11.3.64.

iveness and higher productivity, but it also provides the employees with information about the extent of the plan's success.

The employees' participation in improving operations is achieved through establishing departmental and plant-wide production committees. These groups meet at regular intervals to discuss suggestions submitted from individual employees, and to formulate general plans for improving productivity. Rejected suggestions, or suggestions affecting the plant as a whole, are referred to the plant-wide committee. This group consists of members of top management and the union leadership. They consider suggestions that relate to every phase of the company's operations.

Under the Scanlon plan, what happens to proposals that result in changes? Let us consider several examples:

* At the LaPointe Machine Tool Company, their best and most experienced form grinder was earning $3.57 per hour under the original piecework system. He had no incentive to share his knowledge and skill. After the installation of the Scanlon plan, this operative reorganized his work, took on two helpers, and taught them his skills and methods of doing the job. He also increased his productivity by about 300%.[1]

* At a printing plant, management tried to introduce a conveyor system. The engineers had developed the plans without consulting any of the employees. The system failed to work properly from the start, and there was no interest from the employees in making it work.
  After adopting the Scanlon plan, management decided to try to introduce a conveyor system again, but to handle its introduction in a different manner. A small-scale model of the proposed layout was constructed and shown to the employees. They were encouraged to make criticisms and suggest improvements. From these comments, the joint production committee made modifications to eliminate problems that the engineers had not anticipated. The new system was installed successfully, and was supported with enthusiasm by the employees.[2]

* Later on, we discovered the reason why one of our grinding departments was continually running low on work. We were not

[1] R. W. Davenport, 'Enterprise for everyone', *Fortune*, **41**, No. 1, January 1950, p. 55.

[2] Condensed from G. Shultz, 'Worker participation in production problems', *Personnel*, **28**, No. 3, November 1951, p. 201.

able to compete against other broach[1] companies. This problem was taken up with the workers in the department involved, and the union asked the company to set their prices at a competitive level in order to bring work in. The company was a little reluctant to do so as they showed us some of the large losses which this department had taken. Nevertheless, we still maintained that if the company would go out and get some of this business, we would do all that we could to make it a profitable job. Finally, the company agreed to take another order for these tools and had to bid $17 each below our former manufacturing cost. The order was for 1000 broaches. All workers concerned with this job got together and came forth with their ideas on how the job should be run. Consequently, on the first 100, there was only a slight loss. The remaining 900 were made with a profit of better than 10%.[2]

* One of the pressroom employees pointed out that waste paper was now being crumpled up and thrown in a basket in preparation for salvage. Everyone conceded that, if this paper could be salvaged in flat form, its value would be much higher. Management had been aware of this possible saving but had been unable to enlist the cooperation of the employees in keeping the stock flat. A committee member pointed out the reason for the lack of cooperation: workers felt the foreman was trying to check on them to see how much paper they wasted. Consequently, through various subterfuges they made it impossible for him to police his system. With the suggestion and impetus coming from the employees themselves, however, there was no trouble in getting the waste paper placed in flat form on pallets located at appropriate places in the pressroom.[3]

* I (i.e. a foreman) was in engineering today and they gave me a blueprint of a job coming into the department about two months from now. There are some tough problems on it. I gave a copy to the operators who will be working on the job and asked them to look it over, suggest methods and tools. You'd be surprised at the number of things they can suggest that you'd probably never think of. Then, when the job comes in, I'm ready for it

[1] A type of tool.

[2] F. G. Lesieur (ed.), *The Scanlon Plan: A Frontier in Labor–Management Cooperation*, Wiley, New York: The Technology Press, Cambridge, 1958.

[3] G. Shultz, 'Worker participation in production problems', *Personnel*, **28**, No. 3, November 1951, p. 6.

and so are the operators. Besides, doing it that way lets the operator know he is important. And he is important.[1]

* There is a surprising quantity of proposals for increasing efficiency and eliminating waste which has come from the productivity committees. Over 1000 suggestions have been made so far, and although at the beginning many of the proposals were really disguised complaints, recent months have shown a rise in the proportion of worthwhile ideas. Many of these have been adopted. For example, the line workers in one part of the plant suggested that maintenance holdups would be avoided if the craftsmen did their work during the normal dinner hour. The craftsmen agreed after the management had said that they could take their dinner break at a different time.[2]

Why has the Scanlon plan created an atmosphere of acceptance and support rather than resistance to changes?

* There is an absence of compulsion or threat.

* Employees both suggest and accept changes because they share in the benefits. There is an easily understood and direct reward for implementing changes that result in improvements.

* The adoption of the plan itself and the particular wage formula is arrived at through the process of bargaining.

* A mutality of interest is developed between the employees (and their union) and the management. The company's continued success is perceived by all as the most effective guarantee of their personal security.

* Because of the improvements made in operating effectiveness, the company can compete more successfully in the sale of its products. The resulting increases in its business activity provide an excellent means for absorbing any potentially redundant and surplus employees.

[1] G. P. Shultz and R. P. Crisara, 'The LaPointe Machine Tool Company and United Steelworkers of America', National Planning Association, November 1952.

[2] J. Bourne, 'The Linwood plan: a signpost for labour relations?', *The Financial Times*, London, 11.3.64.

* An environment is created where most employees are highly motivated to expand their knowledge and to increase their skills. Hence, training can be carried on in an atmosphere of enthusiasm and acceptance.

* Discussions and the sharing of all information relevant to the company's operations and business is an essential element in the success of the Scanlon plan. These discussions are carried on at all levels in the organization.

* Typically, the timing of changes is established jointly between the employees and the management.

* Full participation and involvement in making decisions is another essential element in the success of the plan. The entire operation of the plan is based on such participation. Workable suggestions are rewarded by the monthly bonus. Suggestions are rejected only after careful consideration by a group. Rejections are accompanied by full explanations.

* The Scanlon plan can work only if managers and supervisors are able to abandon their traditional prerogatives and attitudes. There is no place for the autocratic or authoritarian manager in a system based on free and open criticism, discussion and consultation. Moreover, management must be willing to share all information openly, and discuss and act upon any topics raised by their employees and by the union.

Douglas McGregor has summarized effectively the relationship between introducing changes and the Scanlon plan.[1]

> The Scanlon plan is a philosophy of organization. It is not a program in the usual sense; it is a way of life—for the management, for the unions, and for every individual employee. Because it is a way of life, it affects virtually every aspect of the operation of the organization. In this fact lies its real significance.
>
> A fair amount of research has pointed up the fact that resistance to change is a reaction primarily to certain methods

[1] F. G. Lesieur (ed.), *The Scanlon Plan: A Frontier in Labor–Management Cooperation*, Wiley, New York: The Technological Press, Cambrige, 1958, pp. 89 and 94.

of instituting change rather than an inherent human characteristic . . . The Scanlon plan minimizes such resistance because it involves people in the process of creating changes rather than imposing it on them. Improvement management is the Scanlon way of life because everyone is interested in improving the ratio.

Significant examples of worker-generated changes in the organization of work are common in Scanlon plan companies. Ironically, these are frequently changes that management tried unsuccessfully to introduce in pre-Scanlon days. Resistance becomes, instead, active instigation. In fact, the Scanlon plan company experience with the change process is one of the most clear-cut examples of the way in which the research-based predictions of social science are fulfilled in practice.

8 Differences in the Perception of Changes

The owner of the axe, as he released his hold on it, said that it was the apple of his eye; but I returned it sharper than I received it.

HENRY DAVID THOREAU

A foolish consistency is the hobgoblin of little minds, adored by little statesmen, philosophers and divines.

RALPH WALDO EMERSON

WE HAVE been discussing changes as they affect two different groups of people: those concerned primarily with introducing and implementing them, and those affected by their consequences. Earlier, we pointed out that in any group affected there will inevitably be a wide range of perceptions of and reactions to the change.

Likewise, there are differences in how a change is perceived by those responsible for its introduction and implementation. Not only do these differences stem from such individual factors as personality and experience, but they also result from the particular organizational role that the person is taking in the changing situation. This role often has a considerable influence both on the way he perceives the change and on his subsequent behaviour. The nature of each role is determined by the forces that derive from the organizational structure and its context.

Of all those responsible for accomplishing changes, there are at least four distinct and different roles: the originator of the change, the manager responsible for its ultimate success or failure, the first- and second-level supervisors directly concerned with the problems of implementation, and the staff specialists available to give advice based on their expert knowledge. From an examination of these roles, we should be able to gain a better understanding of how and why each one influences the viewpoint of its incumbent.

Clearly, it would be fallacious to assume that every supervisor involved in a change would perceive it identically, or that all staff specialists are subject to the same limitations in the way they view changes. Yet, each of these roles seems to have a certain inherent characteristic frame of reference which tends to affect how the incumbents perceive and approach any change. It is as if certain barriers and filters distorted the way in which the incumbents of each role view what is happening in any change. These barriers and filters prevent them from seeing changes objectively. Yet, each role has other characteristics that seem to help the incumbents view certain aspects of a change with unusual clarity.

Whether the role be that of change originator, manager, supervisor or staff specialist, each has its own unique characteristics. These can both distort and clarify the way in which different aspects of changes are perceived. Now let us examine more closely each of these roles and their characteristics.

The Originator of the Change

The originator of any change is the man with the idea. He is the one who sees the need for a change, defines that need, and devises what he believes is the solution to satisfy that need.

Originating a change, like originating any other idea, is a creative act. Creative thought involves a complex fusion of rational and emotional elements. We know little about the mechanisms that underlie creative thinking. We do know, however, that it is often difficult for the originator of an idea to evaluate it objectively.

Like a proud parent, the originator of an idea has a deep emotional attachment to his offspring. He tends to amplify its virtues. He tends to deny or rationalize its faults and limitations. He has a deep and compelling interest in the implementation of his idea. He tends to visualize only success, not failure. He identifies himself with his idea. Its success is his success. Its failure is his failure. Any criticism of his idea, whether it is direct or implied, is often regarded as a criticism of himself.

It is unreasonable to expect the originator of a change to be dispassionate, objective and detached from the process of that change. He can see its beneficial results with great clarity, and he may be unduly optimistic about the magnitude of those benefits. On the other hand, he may underestimate or not wish to face up to the difficulties and problems which must be solved before these benefits can be realized.

It is natural for the originator of a change to want to involve himself deeply in its institution and implementation. He is highly motivated to ensure that success is achieved. His enthusiasm and optimism might prove to be an encouragement and a stimulus to those directly responsible for making the change a success. This same optimism and enthusiasm, however, might also cause the originator to become impatient and irritable when faced with obstacles and difficulties that hinder the progress of the change.

When the originator of a change is involved in its implementation, his concern, typically, is that success be achieved on his terms. That is, his approach and his method must be used. He would probably regard any alternative means or modifications to his method as an implied criticism both of his idea and of himself. He would also tend to feel that any such alternatives would mean a weakening of his approach. Such alternatives would therefore be undesirable. As a consequence, he would probably resist any attempts to modify his original plans.

The kind of behaviour described above is not based on an objective evaluation and logical analysis of what is happening. Instead, it is often quite irrational because it is based on an emotional involvement and identification with one particular course of action.

The originator of a change often makes his greatest contribution in two ways. First, he identifies the problem and the need to change. Second, his proposed solution often points the direction in which action should be taken. But his particular detailed solution or method of achieving the objectives need not necessarily be followed literally. Certain modifications or alterations may become essential because of subsequent events. Yet, in the originator's mind, the objectives of the change are often inextricably bound up with one particular detailed method of accomplishment. It is difficult for him to distinguish between the two.

Herein lies a source of difficulty when the originator of a change is also involved in its institution or implementation. Unlike other members of management, supervision, or members of staff service groups, the originator is often deeply committed to one particular course of action. When the realities of the situation make it desirable or necessary to alter this course, even though the objectives remain unchanged, the originator can himself become highly resistant to change.

We must remember that the role of an originator of change is not a separate organizational function. There is no such position as 'change originator'. Instead, anyone who originates a change is at the same time filling another organizational role: usually that of manager, supervisor or staff specialist. Sometimes, the originator of a change is an operative or a clerk.

How much influence the originator's personal involvement and bias has on the way his ideas are implemented will depend on his formal position in the organization. His opportunity to influence the process of change will be the greatest when he is also the manager responsible for its success. His influence will be less when he is a supervisor, and less still when he is a staff specialist. Those at operative level will have the least influence.

Yet, no matter what his formal organizational position is, the originator's direct involvement in the implementation of his ideas can create problems that can affect adversely the success of the change. This does not apply if the originator can implement the change directly by himself (e.g. an operative who devises a more effective routine in doing his job). But when implementing a change depends on other people for its success, the most effective role for its originator is usually that of an adviser with no direct control over events. As an adviser he could continue contributing ideas while the evaluation of what happens and the taking of decisions are in the hands of those with greater objectivity about the situation.

The Manager

The manager is responsible for instituting and implementing a change, and for its ultimate success or failure. In our discussion of his role, we shall assume at first that he is not the originator of the change, but rather is carrying out someone else's ideas.

When changes must be accomplished within an organization, only the line management can both introduce and implement them. Only they are directly responsible for the labour force, and are in the best position to influence their attitude and behaviour. Only the line managers are in direct control of organizing and accomplishing the work to be done. Only they can make all the necessary decisions on which depend the successful achievement of any change.

What are the forces influencing the manager's thoughts and behaviour in a changing situation? Unlike the originator of the change, whose concern first and foremost is that his ideas are successful, the manager's outlook typically is complicated by several, often conflicting interests. Because he does not have the originator's emotional involvement with the change, he is often able to view it more objectively. He tends to see the problems and difficulties as well as the benefits. His estimate of these benefits may be more conservative than the expectations of the originator.

The manager may have certain doubts or reservations about either or both the objectives of the change and the proposed methods of their accomplishment. These doubts may stem from his more objective evaluation of the situation, or from his greater awareness of the risks involved.

In addition, the manager might be influenced by political considerations. He might fear how he could be affected by the change (particularly his status), or he might be concerned about the consequences of failure to achieve the anticipated benefits.

Also, the manager would often be deeply concerned about the effects of the change on his operations, and most particularly on his subordinates. His expectations of their attitudes and reactions would probably have a significant influence on his own attitudes and reactions. His expectations would, however, depend on the effectiveness of his communications and interactions with his subordinates. If, for example, a manager anticipated that a particular change would be met with strong resistance and would threaten the morale of his workforce, he would be inclined to seek alternative means for accomplishing the desired objectives. If he were sufficiently concerned, he might even attempt to modify the objectives themselves.

The net effect of all this on the manager is for him to develop an attitude towards the change and its expected benefits that is markedly different from that of its originator. The manager would tend to be more sceptical and questioning about the change and its objectives. His expectations of any potential benefits would probably be more modest. Finally, he would tend to be more willing to compromise in altering the methods employed for achieving the change, and even in modifying its objectives.

Very few of these comments, however, would be valid if the manager were also the originator of the change. If such were the case, the manager's thoughts and behaviour would tend to be influenced predominantly by those previously described characteristics of the originator's role.

There is another important point about the manager's role. Because the level of his authority and status in the organization is relatively high, he is in a strong position, while the change is still in the form of a proposal, to influence both its objectives and its method of accomplishment. If he has reservations about either of these, his responsibility is to discuss his objections and recommendations both with his superiors and with the originator of the change. If he believes his position is well founded, his responsibility is to do his utmost to modify either or both the objectives and the method of accomplishment.

When a manager finds himself in the position of having to institute and implement a change about which he has strong doubts and questions, the fact that he is in such a predicament is to a considerable extent his own responsibility. He might find himself in such a situation either because he failed to try altering the course of events, or because he was ineffective in doing so. In practice, such failures often result when the manager decides it would be politically unwise or inexpedient to 'make an issue' of the matter. The consequence of such a politically inspired decision is a manager who is left 'holding the bag'. He is required to accomplish a change about which he may have little conviction and many doubts. Such a conflict can have only adverse effects both on the success of the change and on the future career of the manager himself.

The manager has two important goals with respect to any change. First, he must do all he can before the change is introduced to ensure that its conception is sound. This means that its goals must be well founded, that the expectations of potential benefits are realistic, and that the proposed method of accomplishment is practical.

If the manager is wise, he will try to ensure that the method of accomplishing the change remains open and not fixed. If successful, he will have a maximum of flexibility and the freedom to modify or alter the method should this be made necessary by subsequent events. The manager is well situated to accomplish this first goal, because compared with everyone else involved, he is often in the best position to assess the situation and to evaluate matters objectively. Whether or not he can be effective in accomplishing this first goal depends on his managerial abilities, and in particular on his judgement and on the soundness of his relationships with his peers and superiors.

The manager's second goal is to introduce and implement the change effectively, and to achieve optimum results. In this, his success again depends heavily on his judgement and also on the nature of his relationships with his subordinates. In the final chapter of this book, we shall discuss in detail those managerial abilities particularly relevant to the successful accomplishment of changes.

The Supervisor

The characteristics of the supervisor's role [1] are not unlike those of the role of manager, but they differ somewhat in several significant respects. Like the manager, the supervisor is responsible for instituting and implementing changes. But his area of responsibility is more circumscribed than that of the manager. If the scope of the change is broad, the supervisor may be concerned only with certain particular aspects. On the other hand, if the change is more limited (e.g. a change in the method of work affecting only a single operation), the supervisor's role may be almost identical to that of the manager.

Another point of difference is that, unlike the manager, the supervisor can often escape much of the responsibility should the change be a failure. Although the manager is ultimately responsible for success or failure, it is the supervisor who operates in the front lines. It is he who must cope directly with the reactions of the rank-and-file. Although the supervisor can be blamed in part for any failure to achieve the desired objectives, he can escape this burden by shifting the blame, in turn, on any resistant behaviour by the employees. It would be difficult for his superiors to determine how much this resistance was a consequence of the change itself, and how much it was a result of the supervisor's ineptitude. Thus, a supervisor could easily mask any personal failure behind this screen of uncertainty.

Furthermore, the supervisor is likely to be less objective than his manager about the change. Because of his proximity to both the workers and operations, he cannot escape being influenced strongly by his concern about the effects of the change on both. Any problems and difficulties which he might anticipate would probably loom larger to him than they would do to his manager. Also, the supervisor is often limited in the information he receives and is too remote from whatever benefits might result from a change to be impressed with their desirability and importance. Particularly in changes of broad scope, the supervisor would probably be more

[1] In the term 'supervisor', we mean to include all those in first-line supervision, including foremen.

impressed with the problems and difficulties than he would be with any beneficial results.

Such disproportionate concern with the problems associated with a change is likely to distort the way the supervisor regards that change, and often the way he reacts to it. His commitment to its successful accomplishment, therefore, is often less than that of his manager. His expectations are often aimed at a lower level.

There is still another point of difference between the roles of supervisor and manager. The supervisor's status and freedom to act are at relatively low levels in the organization. Consequently, he is not in a strong position, while the change is still a proposal, to influence either its objectives or its method of accomplishment.

Certainly, if a supervisor has well-founded reservations and recommendations about a change, his responsibility is to discuss these with his manager. But even if he has the courage to do so, his comments would probably be somewhat discounted because his bias would be recognized and his judgement would be more open to question. Any of his objections and recommendations would tend to be taken more seriously during the implementation of the change, because such comments would then be regarded as based on direct experience and facts rather than on apprehensions, predictions and conjecture.

Because the supervisor's status is relatively low and because he often feels more insecure about his position than does his manager, political considerations are frequently a strong influence on the supervisor's judgement and behaviour. He would be less inclined than his manager to differ with his superiors. Consequently, the supervisor is often in the position of having to implement a change about which he has more doubts than confidence.

The supervisor's motivation to achieve optimum results, therefore, is often considerably less than that of the manager, and much less than that of the originator of the change. Of all members of management, the supervisor has the greatest predisposition towards compromise and expediency.

The Staff Specialist

One might expect that of all four roles that of staff specialist would enable its encumbents to be the most objective about a change. After all, they have no direct responsibility for results. They are present to give advice based on their expert knowledge. Whether or not and how this advice is used is the manager's responsibility.

The staff specialist should be able to view the entire situation with almost Olympian detachment.

Yet in his perceptions, the staff specialist often resembles the originator of the change in his lack of objectivity. There are several reasons for this.

Because he is a specialist and has expert knowledge about a particular subject (e.g. work study, accounting, the engineering disciplines, quality control, organization and methods, safety, etc.), he becomes an originator of ideas. These ideas inevitably lead to suggested changes. The staff specialist, therefore, is an originator of change: either the entire change with which he is involved, or certain aspects of it. His role is to analyse the situation, identify problems, think creatively and propose solutions. Once he has begun to offer advice and suggestions, all the characteristics that we formerly attributed to the originator of the change also apply to the staff specialist: emotional involvement with and attachment to his ideas; underestimation of any problems and difficulties; and inflexibility about subsequent attempts to modify his suggestions.

Also, the specialist is often blind to the social and psychological implications of the change as a whole. It is often difficult for him to conceive or to be aware of the problems that might be imposed by the change on the people involved. He can be so engrossed in the technology of the change that he is oblivious to the things troubling them. This problem is intensified when the staff specialist is the originator of major elements of the change. Let us consider two illustrations of what can happen.[1]

* In one situation the staff people introduced, with the best of intentions, a technological change which inadvertently deprived a number of skilled operators of much of the satisfaction that they were finding in their work. Among other things, the change meant that, whereas formerly the output of each operator had been placed beside his work position where it could be viewed and appreciated by him and by others, it was now being carried away immediately from the work position. The workmen did not like this.

  The sad part of it was that there was no compelling cost or technical reason why the output could not be placed beside the work position as it had been formerly. But the staff people who had introduced the change were so literal-minded about their

[1] P. R. Lawrence, 'How to deal with resistance to change', *The Harvard Business Review*, **32**, No. 3, May–June 1954.

ideas that when they heard complaints on the changes from the operators they could not comprehend what the trouble was. Instead, they began repeating all the logical arguments why the change made sense from a cost standpoint. The final result here was a chronic restriction of output and persistant hostility on the part of the operators.

* An industrial engineer undertook to introduce some methods changes in one department with the notion firmly in mind that this assignment presented him with an opportunity to 'prove' to higher management the value of his function. He became so preoccupied with his personal desire to make a name for his particular techniques that he failed to pay any attention to some fairly obvious and practical considerations which the operating people were calling to his attention but which did not show up in his time-study techniques. As could be expected, resistance quickly developed to all his ideas, and the only 'name' that he finally won for his techniques was a black one.

The specialist often believes that the technical aspects of a change should be the sole or primary determinant for its acceptability. His view is that, after all, these technical aspects are based on facts and can be analysed and evaluated objectively. Such matters are the specialist's concern. It is often difficult for him to understand and to accept the idea that the psychological and social effects of the change are what, in most cases, determine the extent of resistance. For the specialist to think in these terms is alien to his outlook. He would consider these psychological and social effects to be essentially irrational because they cannot be identified and measured with precision.

Another problem of the staff specialist's viewpoint is his inclination to underestimate the contribution that can be made by supervision at the lower levels, as well as by operatives, to improving both the method of the change and possibly even its objectives. It is often difficult for a staff specialist to recognize that foremen and operatives are really specialists in their own right, in their experience with operating problems. Because of his more sophisticated appreciation of the technology of the operation, the specialist can often overlook the value of the intimate, practical knowledge that these men possess.

In actuality, anyone with continuous, firsthand experience of operations can aid staff specialists (as well as managers) in two ways. They can often identify practical difficulties or problems with the specialists' ideas, and help to correct these difficulties before they become major issues. Also, they can draw upon their knowledge of the existing social arrangements in the work situation, and point out those elements of the change which might adversely affect these relationships. Thus, they can help to develop improved approaches for accomplishing the change, so that any disruption of the social arrangements will be minimized, thereby increasing the probability of acceptance.

A further problem with many specialists is that they often fail to appreciate the complexities and problems that prevent the rapid accomplishment of changes. Because their position is often somewhat removed from operations, and because their interactions and therefore the amount of information they receive are restricted, they are frequently oblivious to the amount of time that must be taken for those involved to adjust to the change and reach solutions to the problems created. Time is also necessary for learning new skills and for absorbing new knowledge. In addition, time is needed to work out any technical difficulties that were not foreseen. Because of his familiarity with the technology of the change, the specialist often finds it difficult to appreciate why others cannot understand it as readily as he does, and speedily adapt themselves to the new conditions.

When a specialist loses patience with the timing of a change, there can be friction between himself and the managers, supervisors and operatives involved. They may feel that the specialist is exerting pressure on them. The result can be feelings of frustration, antagonism and increased resistance.

Still another problem common to many staff specialists is their difficulty in communicating with those directly involved in the change. A specialist with this problem may adopt one of two approaches in his communications. On the one hand, he might assume that the bases for his ideas and suggestions are so subtle and complicated that it would be futile to attempt their explanation to others, particularly if their education and experience were significantly different from his own. On the basis of this premise, he would tend to oversimplify his explanations and 'talk down' to members of management and to the operatives. On the other hand, he might try to impress them with his brilliance by dazzling them with a highly technical explanation, replete with complex mathematical formulae and data, and technical jargon.

Either approach would create problems. Those who might receive the oversimplified explanation could regard this as an insult to their intelligence, and become infuriated. Those who might be given the full 'scientific' treatment could become confused and frustrated because they were not able to follow the argument. They, too, could become infuriated.

The ability to translate complicated technical material into terms that are readily understandable by laymen is a special skill which few staff specialists possess. The specialist who can do this effectively has patience and understands the frame of reference of his audience.

Sometimes, the staff specialist has additional problems. When he becomes involved in a change, he expects that everyone concerned will resist it blindly. This assumption makes no allowances for any individual differences in attitudes and reactions. When a specialist bases his dealings with people on this attitude, he often provokes the very reaction he expects. When people are treated as if they were intractably stubborn, their ire can be aroused to the extent that they conform to this expectation.

Can the manager do anything to broaden the perspective of the staff specialist so that he can contribute more effectively to the realization of a change? Certainly, there are no simple and rapid solutions to those problems we have described. Many of these difficulties are a consequence of the narrowly focused and circumscribed nature of the specialist's education, training, exeperience and interactions. Adding to these difficulties can be those elements of his personality which caused him to become attracted to a career as a specialist in the first place.

Yet, in time, a manager can help a specialist to broaden his outlook. The manager could ensure that the specialist's relevant interactions with respect to the change are broadened and intensified so that he gains a balanced understanding of the entire problem. If the specialist is over-involved in a particular change, the manager might encourage him to develop an interest in one or more other projects. Thus, his energies and attention could be diffused rather than concentrated. By individual 'coaching' and through personal example the manager could encourage the specialist to become more conscious and appreciative of the contributions and assistance that he might gain from operating personnel. Once the specialist was able to experience directly such help from operatives and foremen, his conversion would be more likely.

Furthermore, it is desirable that the specialist develop an understanding of and an appreciation for those factors which motivate human beings at work. He should learn that those satisfactions which he derives from being creative and productive are the same satisfactions which most people desire to enjoy. Yet, their opportunity to achieve these satisfactions from their work is controlled, in part, by his behaviour towards them. He can come to realize that there is great satisfaction in helping and encouraging others to enjoy the pleasures of being creative. He can also be made to realize that there can be a great personal challenge and reward for him in winning the acceptance of his ideas. Both this challenge and reward can come through achieving a better understanding of and more productive relationships with others. Such an accomplishment can yield satisfactions comparable to those resulting from the generation of new ideas.

Summary

By now, it should be clear that each of the four organizational roles present in any changing situation has particular characteristics. These tend to distort and to colour the judgements made by the incumbents of each role. When an originator, a manager, a supervisor and a staff specialist become involved in a change, each will have his own expectations and his own way of looking at and thinking about that change. These viewpoints can be quite different from one another.

The originator will tend to see the change with the least amount of objectivity. He will be the most optimistic about the resuts, the most impatient about timing and problems, and the most resistant to any subsequent efforts to modify or alter his original ideas.

The manager will tend to be the most objective. He can visualize the benefits and anticipate the problems. Provided that he is not also the originator of the change, he should be able to evaluate the situation as it develops, and make any necessary changes to the method of accomplishment. In his position, he determines the extent of success or failure.

The supervisor is likely to be influened more by whatever difficulties and problems he expects from the change than by any potential benefits. It is not unusual for a supervisor to find himself having to implement a change about which he has more doubts than confidence.

Because the staff specialist is generating suggestions and advice about the change, he often has a bias similar to that of the originator. The narrowness of his specialization often causes him to be insensitive to the psychological and social effects of the change.

In any particular change, there are likely to be wide differences in the motivations towards success of the originator, the manager, the supervisor and the staff specialist. Of these four, the originator is likely to have the strongest desire for success. If the basis for the change is sound, the manager should have the next greatest interest in achieving a successful result. The supervisor's motivations would tend to be considerably less strong. Unless they were deeply involved, the specialists would probably be somewhat indifferent about success.

Finally, we should emphasize that resistance to a change can occur at any level. That is, like the rank-and-file, managers and supervisors too can become resistant. Two factors in particular can cause such resistance. One is the manager's or supervisor's estimates of the political consequences of a change. Their concern is for their status in the organization, both for the present and also for the future. They might also become resistant if they felt pressured into implementing a change in which they had little confidence and much doubt.

Senior management must understand that in bringing about changes they must consider the feelings and needs of their managers and supervisors in the same way that they would expect the feelings and needs of all the workers involved to be considered. Similarly, the manager directly responsible for implementing the change should also consider the feelings and needs of those staff specialists whom he has invited to participate. For any change to succeed, the manager and supervisors directly responsible must first be unified as closely as possible with the originator in their will to accomplish the change with optimum effectiveness. Also, they must accept full responsibility for the ultimate success or failure of that change.

9 A Systematic Approach to Making Changes

The enterprise's demand for the worker's ability to change therefore requires positive action to make it possible for him to change.

PETER DRUCKER

IN THE preceding chapters, we have discussed how people are affected by changes in which they are involved, and how they can react. We have also analysed resistant behaviour and its causes, together with several managerial techniques for minimizing such behaviour. Can we now integrate these ideas and develop a comprehensive and systematic approach for managers to use when they must introduce and implement any change?

Clearly, it would be both impracticable and undesirable to suggest that a rigidly standard approach could or even should be used in any area of managerial activity. There are at least two major reasons for this. Firstly, there are different personal styles of managing. These differences preclude the broad applicability of any single method of approach. Manager A might succeed with the identical method that Manager B employed fruitlessly. That method might have suited A's personal style of managing, as well as his relationships with his superiors, subordinates and peers and the nature of the organizational structure with its cultural beliefs and norms. Because that method might have been unsuitable to B's style, his relationships and the organizational context, B would have felt uncomfortable and unsympathetic towards it. If such were the case, B would have found it difficult to apply that method.

Secondly, a standard method of solving any managerial problem is a useless concept because no single approach can possibly take into account the enormous variability of all the factors present in each unique situation and organization. The facts of organizational life are far too complicated to permit the application of universal methods and solutions. Just as it is impossible to prescribe the single 'proper' method for raising children, so is it also impossible to prescribe managerial formulae guaranteed to produce effective results in every, or even in most, situations.

Yet, although we cannot develop universally applicable methods for managers to use, we can nevertheless offer suggestions to help them improve their ability to cope with changes. Any manager can be helped to develop a systematic approach to the way he carries out changes.

This approach must provide for the identification and consideration of as many as possible of the significant factors that might affect the outcome, before any decisions are made or action is taken. Such thoroughness can serve only to improve the quality of those decisions and the effectiveness of that action. A manager who adopts a more systematic approach to a change will be more likely to anticipate correctly how those involved will react, and thus to cope with their reactions. A more successful implementation of that change will be the inevitable result.

We cannot specify any set of detailed procedures for managers to follow when they carry out changes. We can, however, suggest a number of factors about which they should be concerned, together with a general sequence for their consideration. These factors should be regarded as a kind of guide or checklist. With this, any manager wanting to improve his effectiveness in making changes can ensure that he has overlooked nothing of importance, either in his planning or in his implementation.

Every element of this checklist will not be relevant for all situations. But any manager can use this list to decide at the outset what is of significance in his particular case. He must then assemble the relevant data and make his evaluations, again employing some of the techniques already suggested. Finally, he must decide what action to take.

Broadly, there are at least five phases of managerial action in realizing any change: (a) analysing and planning the change; (b) communicating about the change; (c) gaining acceptance of the required changes in behaviour; (d) making the initial transition from the *status quo* to the new situation; and (e) consolidating the new conditions and continuing to follow up. Let us now consider each of these phases in detail.

Analysing and Planning the Change

Before taking any action to introduce or implement a change, the manager responsible should first devote some time to analysis and planning. In this initial phase, he should have three objectives. His first goal should be to anticipate, in as specific and as detailed terms as possible, what effects the change is likely to have on those involved, and what problems are likely to arise. Such predictions can be framed only in terms of probabilities. The manager's second objective should be to work out in advance answers and solutions to some of the more important anticipated questions and problems. His third goal should be to develop a tentative but detailed plan and timetable for action.

So that the manager can develop plans that are both realistic and workable, he must have from the outset a broad understanding of the basis of the change, its objectives, its scope and its implications. He can develop this understanding by answering a number of questions (listed below) about the change. They should be answered in sufficient detail so that a clear and thorough understanding is reached by all members of management concerned. This analysis must be made before any action is taken to introduce the change itself.

* What are the objectives of the change, both in short- and long-range terms? What is to be accomplished? To what extent are these goals desirable? To what extent are they realistically achievable?

* What is the proposed method for accomplishing the change? How is it to be introduced and implemented? How can this method be distinguished from the objectives of the change? How strong is the commitment to one particular method? Can other methods be used provided that the objectives are achieved?

* What is the justification for making the particular proposed change? What are the expected benefits to be realized? Who is to gain from these benefits? To what extent are these expectations realistic? What are the probabilities for success and failure? Is any change at all really necessary?

* Who originated the idea for the change? What is his motivation for proposing the change? Is he still motivated by these forces?

To what extent will he be directly involved in or able to control the realization of the change? What is the nature of the relationship between the originator of the change and the manager responsible for its success?

* Who else in the organization (other than the originator) is active in supporting the change? How widespread is this support? What are the organizational levels of the supporters of the change, and what are their relationships to the manager responsible for its success?

* By what date must the change be achieved? How flexible is this deadline? How complete must the change be by that date? Would it be possible first to test the change experimentally with a trial group? How long a period of time is available for the introduction and implementation of the change? How justifiable or valid is that target date of completion?

* What is the scope of the change? What are the short-term and longer-term implications? How far-reaching will be the effects of the change (on the way the work is done and organized, on the organizational structure, on the culture)? Who will be directly affected? Who will be affected indirectly? Who will be involved in the introduction and implementation of the change? Who else should be informed about the change and its progress, even though they may not be directly concerned? What will be the effect on the union and at what point ought they to become involved?

* Who is being held responsible and accountable for realizing the expected benefits from the change? What are the sources of assistance the manager can employ in accomplishing the change?

The answers to these questions can be thought out and recorded by the manager himself, alone and in isolation. Many changes are straightforward enough to be handled by a single manager. If such is the case, this process need not occupy more than several hours. Any manager who develops the answers to these questions in a systematic and thorough manner should have a broad appreciation of the background and nature of the change. This understanding can serve as a sound foundation upon which he can then build his subsequent plans for action.

Once he understands the basis for a change, a manager can then go on to estimate its probable effects on those to be involved, together with their probable reactions. This procedure, already described in detail in chapters 3, 4 and 5, is based on the manager's imagined projection of himself into the positions of those likely to be affected by the change. While he regards the change from their viewpoint, the manager can construct two separate lists.

The first list would be made up of all the possible answers that the manager could imagine to the following questions:

* If this change were to apply to me, what questions would I want to be answered about my future circumstances?
* What might I have to fear from the change?
* What might I reasonably expect to lose as a consequence of this change?

The second list would be made up of all the possible answers that the manager could imagine to the following questions:

* If this change were to apply to me, what might I expect to gain from the change?
* How might I benefit from the change?
* What new advantages might I reasonably anticipate as a result of this change?

When only a few people are to be affected, the manager should consider how each individual is likely to react. Thus, he could construct separate lists for each one, taking into account any individual differences in needs, goals, attitudes and behaviour. When, however, the group to be affected is large, it is difficult to consider each individual separately. In these circumstances, the manager's lists must be sufficiently comprehensive to include as many as possible of the more likely reactions.

Once these lists have been compiled, it is then possible to construct one or more balance sheets of estimated losses and gains (see Fig. 4, p. 64). On each sheet, the specific fears and questions, together with the hopes and expected benefits, can be grouped according to their nature. The intensity of feeling about each loss and each gain should be estimated. Also, those feared losses which are a consequence of cultural beliefs should be identified and segregated.

These balance sheets can be analysed by asking the following questions:

* Which fears are primarily a product of individual imaginations and which are more realistically based?

* Which hopes and expected benefits are primarily products of individual imaginations, and which are more realistically based?

* How can those fears and hopes which are imagined and not realistically based be dissipated? What facts and arguments are necessary, and what form should any reassurance take?

* Which questions will require specific and detailed answers? What facts will be necessary so that acceptable answers can be supplied?

* When the realistically based fears are compared with the realistically based expectations, what is the extent of the imbalance?

* If the estimated losses greatly outweigh the estimated gains, is it wise to proceed at all with the change in its present form? How could either the change itself or its method of accomplishment be so modified as to restore some degree of balance between the forecasted losses and gains?

* If the estimated losses outweigh the gains, what action can be taken to minimize the imbalance or, better, to reverse the imbalance? Which losses are likely to be the most significant barriers to the acceptance of the change? Which losses can be eliminated altogether? What offsetting gains can be added?

* Which cultural beliefs are susceptible to being changed? What facts and arguments are required to accomplish such changes?

From analysing the balance sheets in this way, a manager can develop a positive programme for action. He can assemble whatever facts and construct whatever arguments are necessary to answer questions and to dispel groundless fears, hopes and cultural beliefs. He can plan how to communicate these facts and arguments with those concerned. He can modify both the change and its method of accomplishment so that the balance between the forecasted losses and gains can be improved. He can plan and eliminate many of the objectionable aspects of the change. Finally, he can plan and provide rewards to offset those objectionable features of the change which cannot be eliminated.

The final stage of analysing and planning the change is the development of a tentative but specific timed plan for its introduction, implementation and follow-up. Firstly, each distinct task or element of the change should be identified and listed. Next, the dependent elements should be distinguished from the independent ones. Thus, from analysing such a list, the manager should find that some elements must be completed before others are begun. He should also find that other elements can be carried out at any time, because they are independent of the rest.

After this analysis is done, all the elements of the change should be arranged in their proper sequential or parallel relationships. The time needed to complete each element can be estimated. Then, priorities can be assigned to the accomplishment of each task. Naturally, the highest priority should be given to completing those elements which, on further analysis, appear to be critical to the achievement of the entire change. For complex changes with many separate elements requiring long periods of time for completion, the techniques of network analysis (e.g. critical path scheduling or PERT[1]) may be employed to develop the timed plan and to assign the priorities.

It must be recognized, however, that any timed plan constructed at this preliminary stage of the change must necessarily be tentative. Although there must be a general plan for action, its timetable should be sufficiently flexible to enable the incorporation of modifications whenever this becomes necessary.

A timed plan can serve two functions for management. Once constructed, it becomes a master plan for action. As such, it must be considered a dynamic instrument, subject to systematic reviews and revisions. Thus, with a timed plan, management can understand at each step of the change its numerous facets, how they interrelate with one another, and what sequence of action is required. Also, the timed plan is a control tool that management

[1] For a more complete discussion of these techniques, see A. Battersby, *Network Analysis for Planning and Scheduling*, Macmillan: Cleaver-Hume Press, London, 1964.

can use to measure their progress and accomplishment. From periodic comparisons of the actual and the planned status of each element of the change, management can develop detailed pictures of what is on schedule and what is falling behind.

We have already noted that in the initial stage of analysis and planning the manager's task is to develop an understanding of the background of the change and its objectives, scope and implications. This he can accomplish by himself, in isolation. In the subsequent stages of analysis and planning, however, he should not rely entirely upon his own imagination and intelligence in his efforts to anticipate reactions, to plan a programme for minimizing resistance, and to construct a timed plan for action. Instead, he should make these tasks a collaborative effort. He should involve his subordinate supervisors, together with key members of any relevant staff service groups.

Developing these plans through group discussion should have several beneficial effects:

* The quality of these plans, in terms of their comprehensiveness and accuracy in anticipating future events, should be enhanced because a variety of viewpoints and knowledge will have been brought to bear upon the problems. There is a strong likelihood that plans developed in this way will be realistically based.

* Because all relevant supervisors and staff specialists will have been involved in the discussions from the start, they should develop a thorough understanding of the change and its implications. This should help to minimize any reservations or doubts that they might otherwise have had about the change.

* Because supervisors and members of staff groups will have participated in planning the change, their commitment to it and its objectives should approach that of the manager. Thus, all those responsible should be unified and consistent in their management of the change.

* The staff specialist's typically narrow perspective should become broadened. As a consequence, he should become more flexible and understanding in the way he deals with those affected by the change.

The analysis and planning phase of a change should be completed before any overt action is taken actually to institute it. Thus, management shoud be prepared beforehand to cope with any resistance. They should have a clear concept of what is to be accomplished and why. They should understand how the change is likely to be perceived by the people affected and by the union. Because management will have anticipated many of the problems, they should be prepared to meet these difficulties with possible solutions. With such preparation, management can improve the probability of acceptance of the change by those on whom its ultimate success is most dependent. Thus, the time management invest in analysing and planning the change should pay rich dividends during their subsequent implementation of it.

Communicating About the Change

The next phase of any change should be a period of communication during which management thoroughly discuss it and its implications with those affected and involved (including the union). Much of this communication should be carried out before any action is taken to introduce the actual changes.

In this phase, a manager should have two objectives. He should ensure that all those involved develop as complete an understanding as possible about the reasons for the change and its objectives and anticipated benefits, about the intended method (or alternative methods) of approach, about the proposed timetable and plan for action, and about how they are likely to be affected. Also, the manager should try to assess both individuals' and the union's reactions by identifying as many as possible of their specific questtions, beliefs and fears about the change.

Essentially, this communication must be a two-way process. The manager and his supervisors must transmit information about the change to everyone concerned with what is to happen. This information should be primarily factual, but it may also contain some realistically based conjecture and predictions. In addition, however, management must do some listening. They must listen so that they can evaluate the effectiveness of their communications by assessing how much understanding has been achieved. Also, they must listen to the comments and ideas expressed about the change. From these can be determined the employees' and the union's true attitudes and reactions, not all of which will have been anticipated. From such two-way communication, both the employees and management should learn what to expect.

This process should be of benefit to everyone involved in the change. By understanding what is to happen, the employees should be better able to adjust to the new conditions. Also, they (together with the union) can influence the course of events before these actually occur. This is especially important if there are elements of the change which might affect them adversely.

By gaining a preview of the employees' and the union's reactions to the change, management can modify those aspects which might otherwise have proved objectionable, or introduce compensating factors. Management can benefit in another way from discussing the change in advance with their employees and with the union. Because of their involvement in discussions, these employees, together with the union, will probably feel less intense about resisting the change. By gaining prior knowledge of what will be happening to them, they would, in time, tend to accommodate themselves to this eventuality (see chapter 6, p. 80. Also, the union's institutional requirements for recognition and continued survival would be satisfied in part.

Clearly, for management, their employees and the union to realize these benefits management must be willing to share as much as possible of the information about the change. True understanding can be based only on full knowledge of the relevant facts. Withholding or distorting information about the change will, in most instances, prove to be more harmful than beneficial to management. If they are apprehensive about sharing certain information in advance, they should analyse and compare the risks with the potential benefits before they finally reach a decision (see chapter 6, p. 78).

In a changing situation, communication should be maintained with as many of the people concerned and as extensively as possible. Communication must be not only with those directly affected, but also with those on the periphery of the change. For example, members of relevant staff groups should be included. Also, people doing related jobs may regard a change in another area as a prelude to what may later happen to them. In such instances, these persons too should be included. Finally, both national and local union officials should be involved from the outset of the change, if it is at all relevant to matters about which the union is concerned.

Communication with all these people can be accomplished most effectively through discussions with individuals and groups. However, management should also consider using any other written and oral media that might help improve understanding of what is to happen (see chapter 7, pp. 94–99).

This intensive programme of communications should begin with the completion of the analysis and planning phase of the change. The programme should be continued throughout the entire change until its objectives are met. No action should be taken to introduce any actual changes until there has been sufficient discussion to reach general agreement that some kind of change is necessary, and that one or more of the approaches being discussed will probably produce the desired results. When a change is complex with far-reaching implications, management should plan their timetable so that sufficient time is allowed for communications to be thorough and complete.

Considerable time is required particularly for changing deeply rooted cultural beliefs and mistaken notions. These beliefs must be altered before the way can be paved for the acceptance of new ideas and practices. Thus, cultural beliefs can best be challenged and altered during the communications phase of a change.

Throughout this period, all references to the particular methods that might be employed to achieve the intended changes should be framed in terms of possibilities and proposals. *No doubts should be allowed to persist about the desirability or inevitability of realizing management's objectives.* On the other hand, the actual methods for their accomplishment should at this point be perceived as proposals, subject to further alteration and modification. Such flexibility is essential if those involved are to believe that their comments and suggestions will be considered seriously.

Management can be flexible about their approach only if they are able to distinguish clearly between their objectives and how these are to be accomplished. They should be able to complete the development of the particular method during the next phase of the change. This method should evolve from a proposal towards a more definite plan during the discussions of the communications phase.

The principal function of the communications phase is to enable those involved (and the union) to accustom themselves to the idea that a change is needed, and that it will soon be taking place. Attention should be focused on the objectives of the change and their justification. At the outset of the communications phase, it should be made clear that precisely how the change is to be accomplished has not yet been crystallized into its final form. This, therefore, is a proper subject for discussion and consideration. By the latter stages of the communication phase, all concerned should understand why the change is necessary, what is to be achieved, what are some alternative methods of approach, and what are the more important problems that might result from each of these alternatives. Thus, at the close of the communications phase, they should be close to agreement on the most desirable method for accomplishing the change.

Gaining Acceptance of the Required Changes in Behaviour

The next phase of a change is the period during which agreement is reached on what specific alterations are required in the employees' behaviour to accomplish the transition from the *status quo* to the desired conditions. These behavioural changes necessary for the transition are determined by the particular method management select to accomplish the desired objectives, together with the nature of the objectives themselves. Agreement on these should be reached between management and a significant majority of those affected by the change.

It is difficult to define exactly when this phase begins and ends. It starts some time during the latter stages of the communications phase, when many have begun to understand and accept what is about to happen and in particular how they are likely to be affected. This phase ends when a general agreement has been achieved about how much and what kinds of behavioural changes are required to accomplish the transition from the existing conditions to the desired situation.

A manager can secure agreement to a particular method of change in one of several ways. He can apply persuasion and offer rewards. Alternatively, he can reach agreement through negotiation and bargaining. Or, he can invite people to participate in making some of the decisions about how the change is to be accomplished. Finally, any combination of these approaches can be used.

The particular approach chosen should depend on the special circumstances of each case. Persuasion and rewards are appropriate for situations where the manager has already decided that the change can best be achieved only by one particular method. He might also negotiate and bargain to gain acceptance of that one method, especially if there is a union involved and the change is relevant to the labour agreement. However, if he chooses to bargain, he must be prepared to compromise and modify his original ideas.

When it is possible to achieve the change by a variety of methods, the manager may involve the people affected. He may invite them to participate in making some of the decisions about how the change is to be carried out. Participation is effective when the manager is open-minded about how the change might be accomplished, and when there is a choice of alternative approaches. Even when the manager is committed to a single method of carrying out the change, he can nevertheless combine participation with either persuasion or bargaining, provided that there are some elements of the change that could be accomplished in more than one way.

Whatever approach the manager takes, its effectiveness depends on how much discussion takes place. Discussions with everyone concerned must be carried on continuously throughout the change. These discussions should begin at the start of the communications phase and should continue until agreement has been reached on how to proceed with the actual transition. Discussion is the best method for developing an understanding of the change and its implications. Discussion is also an excellent means for ensuring that most of the problems that might later have caused resistance are identified and solved.

Whatever approach a manager chooses to secure agreement, special personal problems will inevitably arise in discussions. These will be individual problems and will not apply to the group as a whole. These problems stem from the conflict between a person's own needs and goals and the effects of the change. The manager can solve such problems if he remains sufficiently flexible in his attitude and approach. Thus, provision can be made for any differences in individual circumstances. He must be able to reconcile what is fair to the person with the problem and what is equitable for the group as a whole. In so doing, the manager should bear in mind that a uniform approach for all is often neither equitable nor fair. Whenever exceptions and modifications are made to accommodate individual needs, these can be understood and accepted by the group if they perceive these exceptions as reasonable.

In most changes, the manager should begin the transition from the status quo *to the new conditions only after a consensus of agreement has been reached about the method of this transition. This agreement can be achieved through the use of rewards, through bargaining, through participation, or through some combination of these approaches. If the transition is attempted before such agreement has been reached, the manager is risking an increased resistance to the change and a lessened probability that the potential benefits will be fully realized.*

Making the Initial Transition

In any change, the next distinct phase is the initial translation from the existing to the new situation. The prior phases of planning, communications and gaining agreement should all preface the actual change itself. Only after these preparatory phases have been successfully completed should management then begin to introduce the specific changes.

Just before the start of the transition, the timed plan for the change (previously developed in the planning phase) should again be reviewed. The manager should question and re-evaluate the originally established final date of completion to determine whether or not it is still realistic and achievable. He should consider whether or not it might be possible or desirable to test out the method of transition on a trial basis. This may be done either by using an experimental group before involving everyone in the change, or by setting up a specific trial period for all involved before the change is finally established as definite. It is extremely important that the target date for completing the change be set so that the manager will not be hindered by any arbitrary deadlines from remaining flexible in his choice of method for handling the transition. Furthermore, there must be sufficient time for finding effective solutions to most of the problems that are certain to arise with the progress of the change.

Once the manager has determined how to handle the transition, he must ensure that everyone involved is briefed on what is to take place. Carefully planned presentations should help to crystallize everybody's understanding of what to expect, why it is to happen, and what the effects should be. Furthermore, these briefings should help them establish what their roles will be during the transition period and afterwards in the new situation.

If new knowedge and skills are required by the change, training activities should be designed and implemented. The objectives of this training must derive from the particular demands made on those involved by the changed circumstances. Such training should not only prepare each person to carry out his responsibilities more effectively, but it should also help him reduce any fears and doubts about his ability to cope with his new responsibilities.

Often, the managers and supervisors have as great a need for both briefing and training as do the operatives and staff. The same can be said of key union members and officials. In complex changes, sufficient time must be scheduled for such training activities before any actual changes are instituted. Time invested in this manner will often yield rich dividends when the benefits from the change are finally measured.

During the transition, more careful and thorough supervision is required than is needed during more stable periods of operation. Many unforeseen problems inevitably arise. Usually, the first-line supervisor is the most appropriate person to answer questions, solve problems, and call for any required staff assistance. He is, in fact, the central link for all communications about the progress of the change during the transition period. He must, therefore, be on the scene and readily accessible. First-line supervisors should therefore spend the greatest proportion of their time at the scene of the change. They should, however, regard themselves more as sources of assistance than as order-givers. The manager, too, should devote more time than normal to acquainting himself with what is happening 'on the shop floor' during the transition period.

We have already emphasized that any required staff specialists should be involved as early as possible during the planning phase of the change. The manager must help them understand the objectives and reasons for the change. They should be kept informed about its progress and about any problems arising as well as about any modifications to the method of change. Because they have contributed ideas and recommendations about both the methods and even the objectives of the change, they are often as deeply concerned about what happens as are those directly affected. If the manager can involve staff specialists in participating directly in formulating some of the decisions about the change, he will ensure that full benefit will be gained from their contributions. By fulfilling the staff specialists' needs in this way, the manager will ensure that their cooperation will continue both during this change and in future changes as well.

During the transition period, the manager must remain continually informed about what is happening at the scene of the change. Up-to-the-minute information is needed if he is to modify the method of approach. Such modifications may become necessary if unforeseen problems arise, or if it appears that better results are achievable through an approach different from the original.

To ensure a constant flow of timely information about the progress of the change, the manager should use several techniques. He should discuss the situation frequently with his first-line supervisors. Also, he should seek opinions and comments from any staff specialists directly involved. He should discuss progress with union representatives. Finally, he should visit the scene of action with sufficient frequency to gain a first-hand appreciation of what is happening. During such visits, he can chat informally with the people directly concerned with making the changes. In this way, he will be in the best possible position to take immediate corrective action should this be necessary.

The transition from the status quo *to the new conditions should begin only after some agreement has been reached on the method of change. The manager should allow sufficient time to make the change on a trial basis, and to solve any unforeseen problems. Briefings and training for supervision, staff, union representatives and operatives should precede the start of any changes. During the transition the supervisors, and to a lesser extent the manager, should spend a considerable portion of their time at the scene of the change so that questions and problems can be resolved without delay. Full benefit can be gained from the contributions of staff specialists by involving them deeply in the planning and conduct of the change. Throughout this phase, the manager must remain well informed about progress so that he can make any necessary modifications to the method of change.*

Consolidation and Follow Up

In any change, the final phase is the consolidation of the new conditions and the continued follow-up of events after the initial transition is complete. Follow-up should continue until the success of the change has been ensured.

Simply because the transition period may have been accomplished smoothly, with few difficulties, the manager should not assume that the change has been an unqualified success. Many unexpected problems can arise later after the initial changes have been made. The planned change might result in subtle secondary effects that may not become apparent for some time. Also, what might appear to be a successful change at the outset might later prove to be a failure because of the effects of subsequent reactions to the new conditions, or of other unforeseen factors.

To ensure that the objectives of a change are fully realized, the manager must institute follow-up procedures that are both systematic and thorough. He must see to it that his first-line supervisors continue to be on the lookout for any signs of difficulty. Also, they must continue to be at the scene of the change with sufficient frequency to correct any misunderstandings and questions that are certain to arise about the new conditions of work.

Furthermore, the manager should ensure that the staff specialists continue their involvement in the change until they can make no further useful contributions. After the initial transition, they can continue to study and report on the progress of the change, as well as to submit their recommendations about any further modifications and refinements.

Also, the manager should institute a procedure whereby he receives regularly scheduled reports, both oral and written, from his first- and second-line supervisors as well as from any staff specialists who remain involved. These reports should draw comparisons between the actual and the planned progress made towards the objectives of the change. The actual accomplishments realized should be described quantitatively with as much objectivity as possible. The prudent manager should supplement this information by conducting informal interviews with key persons directly involved in the change. By chatting with operatives, staff specialists, members of supervision and union representatives, the manager should be able to gain valuable first-hand perceptions of the situation.

Such a systematic follow-up procedure will inevitably reveal the existence of additional problems. With an accurate and timely knowledge of the situation, the manager can act swiftly and decisively. He can either initiate further detailed studies of the areas of difficulty, or he can modify the relevant elements of the change.

During the follow-up phase of the change, the manager should be able to determine the extent to which the anticipated results and benefits have been realized. The effects of the change should be defined and measured as objectively and as specifically as possible. The results can then be compared with earlier expectations. Similarly, any identifiable secondary effects of the change should also be analysed. A final assessment can then be made of the degree of success, together with the reasons either for it or for the lack of it.

From such a review, management can learn lessons from which they can improve their effectiveness in introducing and implementing future changes. In addition, they may discover that, with further immediate action, increased benefits are achievable from the change just 'completed'.

Throughout the change, the manager must keep clearly in his mind those objectives that justified it from the outset. He should feel free to modify or alter the original plan if a better realization of the objectives would result. Just as the manager would wish his employees to remain open-minded and flexible in their attitudes towards the change, so should he also try to remain open-minded and flexible about the possibility of changing his own ideas and approaches to accomplishing that change. Such personal flexibility would be a major element in the success achieved.

To ensure that full benefits from a change are realized, the manager must institute systematic and thorough follow-up procedures. He must be alert to unexpected secondary- and after-effects. He must continue to give close attention to the progress of events so that he can remain fully informed. He must ensure that both the results of the change and the way in which they were achieved are evaluated completely and objectively. The manager can himself contribute greatly to success if he remains flexible about changing the methods used for realizing the change.

Summary: A Case Study

Recently, in Great Britain, there was concluded a change of extremely broad scope with far-reaching implications. In its accomplishment were embodied almost all the concepts we have been describing. This change was the negotiation and implementation of a radically different agreement on labour productivity at the Fawley Refinery of the Esso Petroleum Company, Limited. The development and subsequent implementation of this agreement is described and analysed in detail by Alan Flanders of Oxford University.[1]

Through systematic application of those principles of managing changes outlined in this chapter, a group of managers brought about the acceptance of an entirely different way of working, a way that represented a radical departure from past traditions and practices not only at the refinery but also in British industry. How was this complicated and difficult change accomplished?

Firstly, let us summarize management's objectives. The change was initially stimulated by an economic need: to raise labour productivity as a key element in a more general programme to improve operating efficiency. Soon, however, management had formulated two other objectives of a different kind, objectives concerned with the institutional and cultural aspects of the industrial society at the refinery. One of these objectives was to make labour relations

[1] A. Flanders, *The Fawley Productivity Agreements*, Faber & Faber, London, 1964.

more responsible and constructive, and to create an environment that would emphasize the common interests of management and the unions in improved working methods and in organization. The other objective was to change the attitudes of all employees towards change itself. An effort was to be made to modify those prevailing beliefs and values held both by management and by the workers that tended to be barriers in the path leading to the adoption of new attitudes.

During a two-year period devoted to the planning and communications phases of this change, three things happened. Firstly, a series of very specific proposals were developed defining the desired changes in working methods and practices. Secondly, the entire management structure was simplified and strengthened. Thirdly, everyone involved in this change (including the union) had the opportunity to discuss the proposed changes extensively (initially in general terms and later more specifically) and to gain an understanding of what was to take place and why.

Briefly, the proposed changes in working practices and methods can be summarized as follows. It was proposed that the job of craftsman's mate be eliminated, and all incumbents deployed to other work. Also, it was proposed that a group of existing demarcation practices related to inter-craft flexibility be relaxed so that minor maintenance work could be transferred to process workers, and so that slinging and rigging work could be done by various craftsmen. Furthermore, management were to have greater freedom in their use of supervision, so that craft groups would take orders from any supervisor without regard for his particular craft. In addition, a number of traditional refinery conventions were to be modified. Unproductive time allowances such as those for walking, washing and set tea breaks were to be abolished. Special payments for heat and dirt were to be discontinued. There was to be a dramatic reduction in the number and variety of different pay rates. Finally, the amount of overtime worked on a continuing, regularly scheduled basis was to be reduced from an average of 15–18% to 2%.

To secure the workers' agreement to these changes, management proposed to offer three benefits and one guarantee. One of these benefits was a reduction in the normal basic working week from 42 to 40 hours. Another was the dramatic reduction in the total hours worked each week. Finally, there was to be a significant increase in basic pay rates so that, even after most of the overtime had been eliminated, employees' take-home pay would be greater than it had been at the outset. In addition to these benefits, a pledge was to be made that no one would be made redundant as a consequence of these changes. This pledge was possible because it was feasible to reduce the amount of work being done by subcontractors and because the refinery was in a period of expansion.

After a five-month period of hard bargaining, the union (and the employees) agreed to most of the detailed proposals. During the following two years, the provisions of this new agreement were implemented. What were the results?

The economic results are the easiest to define. In the maintenance departments, the productivity of the individual worker rose more than 50% over the two years following the negotiation of the new agreement. In the process departments, individual productivity increased about 45%. In return for this, the total take-home pay of the workers rose about 21%, and their work week was shortened by about 11%.

The success with which the institutional objectives were achieved is far more difficult to evaluate. Let us quote Mr. Flanders:

> There were certain significant changes in the relations between management and unions at Fawley, which can be conveniently summarized under three heads. First, labour relations acquired a greater formality in that they were governed by more explicit and less flexible rules. Second, the shop stewards' influence on union negotiations was enhanced. Third, rivalry among the three main union groups . . . as represented by the CUC (i.e. the group of crafts unions) and the TGWU (i.e. Transport and General Workers Union) Shift and Day branches . . . was intensified.
>
> It is evident that together (the above changes) they subjected the relations between management and the unions to new stresses and strains. Growing formality made for less give-and-take and ease of accommodation in daily relations. The stewards' augmented influence tended to make union negotiations more protracted and complex. The intensification of rivalry among the different union groups had the same effect, and in addition produced tensions that hampered consistent settlements for the refinery as a whole. The conclusion is inescapable that the immediate effect of the Blue Book and its successor (the local term for the group of specific changes) was to make labour relations more conflict-prone . . . in the sense of rendering them more liable to the confrontation of opposed

> interests or viewpoints. By enlarging the subject matter of formal collective bargaining, and by disturbing settled relationships and accepted comparisons, they extended the range of possible disagreements between the two sides and among the union representatives themselves.
>
> . . . Peace in industry is most easily achieved by avoiding change . . . at any rate change that is likely to meet resistance. Had this been the supreme consideration for Fawley management, the Blue Book proposals would never have been formulated. Managements that engage in productivity bargaining have to be prepared to devote more, not less, of their time to labour relations and to expect that their tasks will become more onerous and exacting.
>
> Since an evaluation of labour relations cannot be based upon the avoidance of conflict, it follows that its increase at Fawley was not necessarily a sign that labour relations there were deteriorating. On the contrary, the absence of any costly stoppages when sharper conflicts had to be resolved could rather be taken as evidence of their improvement. The ingenuity of management and union representaives in finding the workable compromise that would satisfy their constituents was being subjected to a severer test and, on the whole, emerged triumphant.[1]

Mr. Flanders found it more difficult to assess the extent to which management was successful in its third objective of changing attitudes towards change.

> The conversion of top management could be directly observed and tested in many conversations. It appeared to be fairly complete. How the middle and lower levels of management viewed the experiment was much more difficult to ascertain. Such evidence as exists points to a good deal of scepticism about its value and to reservations about particular changes in working practices.[2]

As for the accomplishment of any changes in craft and non-craft workers' attitudes towards change, Mr. Flanders suggests that only slight inroads were made in modifying their traditional attitudes towards lines of craft or trade demarcation, the central problem in many of the changes that were carried out.[3]

[1] A. Flanders, *The Fawley Productivity Agreements*, Faber & Faber, London, 1964, pp. 199 and 206.

[2] *Ibid.*, p. 210. [3] *Ibid.*, p. 212.

How was it possible for management to accomplish successfully such a radical series of changes, many of which were in direct conflict with prevailing cultural beliefs and traditional working practices and habits? There is no simple answer. Certainly, the nature of the economic climate and the generally good relations which existed between management and the workers were important factors. But perhaps one of the more significant reasons for management's success was that they approached the accomplishment of these changes in a planned and systematic manner. Let us examine more closely the elements of their approach.

Management's initial attitude was one reason for the success of the changes. Senior management perceived and accepted the view that it was management's responsibility to change the union's restrictive practices and to reduce overtime. Management understood that if any changes were to be made it was up to them to seize the initiative and not up to the union to do so. Also, management believed that any benefits from increases in individual productivity should be shared between the company and its employees. Thus, management were willing to offer the workers a fair reward for their contribution towards higher productivity.

Another element in the success of the change was management's early appreciation of the concept that cultural change was a necessary prerequisite to institutional change. Thus, if overtime was to be reduced, if the jobs of craftsmen's mates were to be eliminated, and if traditional lines of craft demarcation were to be relaxed, then it was necessary first to challenge and to change a number of deeply rooted cultural beliefs. Many workers, union officials and even members of supervision had to review their longheld beliefs and question their validity. As a consequence of management's grasp of these concepts, they were able to plan and carry out a systematic and comprehensive attack on these beliefs, prior to introducing any changes and starting any negotiations with the union.

A further factor in the success of the changes was the amount of planning that preceded the union negotiations and the introduction of the changes. About one year was devoted to a series of comprehensive and detailed studies of the original situation, to the design of those changes desired, and to the development of a general strategy for their achievement. During this planning phase, the objectives for the changes were clearly defined. Also, the specific proprosals for the changes were developed in great detail. The clear definition of these proposed changes facilitated the subsequent discussions held with both the workers and with the union, and minimized ambiguities and misunderstandings. Management were able to forecast the effects of the changes on those involved, and to estimate how people would react. As a result, management were able to identify beforehand, the main potential sources of resistance to the proposed changes, and to devise a means for minimizing this resistance.

This means was comprised of three distinct elements. Two of these were in the form of rewards that management offered to persuade their employees to change their traditional work habits. One of these rewards was a dramatic decrease in the total hours worked per week. The other was an equally dramatic increase in basic pay. Not only was this pay rise sufficient to offset any possible losses in weekly take-home pay that might otherwise have resulted from the reduction in the number of hours worked, but it was also designed to result in a significant increase in this weekly pay. The third element of management's plan to minimize resistance was to provide positive protection from the workers' strongest fear, that of redundancy. This protection took the form of a pledge that there would be no redundancy as a consequence of the proposed changes.

Yet another factor that contributed to the success of the changes was the amount of communication between management and those involved in the changes, both prior to and during the negotiations with the union, and prior to the actual introduction of any changes. More than one year was devoted to the communications phase of the changes. During this period, management used virtually every possible means to communicate with the supervisors, the workers, and with key union officials. The means most frequently employed by far was face-to-face discussions both with individuals and with groups. In these discussions, cultural beliefs were identified, held up to examination and challenged. Also, the general nature of some of the more fundamental proposals was suggested and discussed. Later, once negotiations had begun, the specific proposals were discussed at length with all employees, who were then encouraged to explore their broader implications. In these discussions, consultation, and to a lesser extent participation, took place. By the end of the negotiations with the union, almost everyone concerned had reached some understanding of what was proposed and why, and what the effects were likely to be. Furthermore, a general acceptance of most of the key proposals had already been achieved prior to the completion of negotiations.

Still another essential factor in the success of the changes was senior management's realization and implementation of a concept: that as a prerequisite to the introduction of any changes, it was first necessary to strengthen management's effectiveness at all levels within the organization. Consequently, during the first year while the changes were being planned, management were also improving their structure and organization. The objectives of this exercise were twofold. Firstly, managers and supervisors at all levels were to accept full responsibility for managing their subordinates. This meant that many personnel matters, formerly left to the care of staff specialists, were to be handled directly by the managers and supervisors themselves. This also meant that managers and supervisors were to become deeply concerned with establishing relationships with their subordinates that would be characterized by mutual respect and trust.

The other objective of the programme to improve management organization was that management should assume full responsibility for determining labour policy. Thus, the managers and supervisors were the ones to decide on the specific proposals for the changes in working practices, and on the methods for their accomplishment. The managers and supervisors were the ones to conduct the discussions of those changes with the men and with the union officials. Also, the managers were the ones to direct and conduct the negotiations with the union.

The management organization was improved by several fundamental changes. The organization structure itself was simplified by a reduction in the number of levels in the heirarchy between the workers and the refinery manager, and also in the number of supervisors. The managers' and supervisors' salaries were increased, so that a proper incentive and reward could be introduced for the increased managerial competence and skills now required. Simplifying the organizational structure shortened and made more effective the lines of communication at all levels. There was a deliberate increase in the delegation of both responsibilities and the freedom to carry them out. This was particularly true of the management of people. Finally, there was a planned effort to involve superivsors and managers at all levels in discussing and solving the enormous number of problems presented by the impending changes. As a consequence of their involvement and participation, they developed a genuine team spirit. This, in turn, led to a unified understanding of and approach to solving these problems, as well as confidence that, no matter how difficult, these problems could be overcome.

Without this development and strengthening of the management and supervisory team, it is doubtful that the productivity proposals could have been introduced successfully. Certainly, neither the planning nor the communications phases of the changes could have been carried out with such telling effect. And even if the changes had been negotiated with the union officials, it is doubtful that they could have been implemented successfully without these improvements in the management organization.

Another factor in the success of these changes was the flexibility of the timetable. Senior management did not impose an arbitrary deadline for the start or completion of negotiations, or for the full implementation of the changes themselves. They realized from the outset that a great deal of time was necessary to plan for these changes, and to prepare the ground for their acceptance. Consequently, the timing of the negotiations was determined by the actual progress made during the communications phase of the changes. Sufficient time was taken during every phase for accommodation to the idea of change to play a significant role. The climate of employee opinion towards the proposals was the primary determinant for establishing the start of the negotiations.

One last factor that contributed to the success of the changes is worthy of mention. This was management's realism in their approach to the bargaining process. They understood that to gain something they had to be prepared to give something in return. The extent of the wage increases, the pledge of no redundancy, and the abandonment of at least one of their key proposals were all illustrations of management's attitude. Furthermore, a number of modifications and compromises were made to the original proposals during the process of negotiation. The final changes agreed by the union differed in some respects from the original list of management's proposals.

These extremely difficult changes were accomplished in the face of seemingly impossible obstacles. Success was a direct consequence of management's adoption of a planned approach that was comprehensive, systematic and thorough. Also, success was achieved because of the enormous emphasis on discussion with everyone concerned. Finally, success was accomplished because structural changes were made in the organization and an effective and unified management team was developed. This team was capable of providing the high quality of supervision required throughout the change, from its communications phase through its transition period and concluding with its follow-up and consolidation.

10

Implications for Managerial Competence

A State which dwarfs its men, in order that they may be more docile instruments in its hands even for beneficial purposes . . . will find that with small men no great thing can really be accomplished.

JOHN STUART MILL

A state without the means of some change is without the means of its conservation.

EDMUND BURKE

THROUGHOUT THIS book, we have emphasized that the manager, together with his subordinate supervisors, must bear the burden of responsibility for achieving successfully the full benefits from any change. But the route to this success contains many barriers and pitfalls. To overcome these obstacles is often difficult. To solve some of the problems can be at times almost impossibe. Occasionally, management must settle for results that are less than what might have been potentially possible.

Enormous demands are made of managers and supervisors when they introduce and implement changes. Probably no other managerial task is more difficult. What are the implications of this for those required to manage? What demands must they be able to fulfil? And what kind of an environment is most likely to stimulate the development and application of the necessary abilities?

Necessary Managerial Abilities

Let us consider initially what demands are made of a manager or supervisor by the task of carrying out a change. To maximize his chances for success, what must he be able to do?

He must be able to understand the full implications of the impending change. He must be able to identify its objectives and grasp the nature of its probable effects. He must be able to imagine himself in the positions of the people to be affected, and view the change through their eyes. He must be able to visualize what they might fear and regard as losses, as well as what they might hope to gain from the change. He must be able to identify any prevailing cultural beliefs that might be in conflict with the change. He must be able to analyse probable attitudes and forecast likely reactions. He must be able to predict with some accuracy the nature and extent of any resistance, and then plan how such resistance could be minimized.

Any manager able to perform all these tasks effectively must have both intelligence and imagination above the norm. Furthermore, he must have a mind trained to approach problems analytically and logically, with a method that embodies systematic planning.

Furthermore, the manager who is to be effective in accomplish ing changes must have a general attitude towards others (and towards his subordinates in particular) that is characterized by confidence, consideration and understanding.

> (Such a manager) has a relatively high opinion of the intelligence and capacity of the average human being. He may well be aware that he is endowed with substantial capacity, but he does not perceive himself as a member of a limited elite. He sees most human beings as having real capacity for growth and development, for the acceptance of responsibility, for creative accomplishment. He regards his subordinates as genuine assets in helping him fulfil his own responsibilities, and he is concerned with creating the conditions which enable him to realize these assets. He does not feel that people in general are stupid, lazy, irresponsible, dishonest or antagonistic. He is aware that there are such inidividuals, but he expects to encounter them only rarely.
>
> The climate of the relationship created by such a manager will be vastly different. Among other things, he will probably practice effective delegation, thus providing his subordinates with opportunities to develop their own capabilities under his leadership. He will also utilize them as resources in helping him solve departmental problems. His use of participation will demonstrate his confidence in them.[1]

[1] D. McGregor, *The Human Side of Enterprise*, McGraw-Hill, New York, 1960, p. 140.

Also, the manager must be skilled in communicating with people at all levels in the organization, whether they be workers, staff specialists, senior managers, or even union officials. He must be a good listener, so that he can test out their reactions to the various elements of the change. He must be able to use skilfully the mechanisms of both individual and group discussions, so that those involved can develop understanding, and so that he can identify for himself those potential problems for which solutions can be found. He must also be able to make the best use of other, more formal means of communicating, and, in particular, those employing the written word.

In addition, the manager must be persuasive in his approach to subordinates, superiors, staff specialists and union officials. In a logical and convincing manner he must be able to organize and marshal those arguments that support the need for the change, as well as for one particular approach to its accomplishment. He must be able to present and develop his arguments so as to persuade those involved to accept and support the change and a method for its realization. Similarly, he must be able to convince his superiors when it is necessary to make certain modifications to the method of change, and possibly even to its objectives. He might also have to persuade senior management that it would be desirable to offer certain rewards so that some of the unavoidable losses from the change might be counterbalanced.

Moreover, the manager must be systematic and thorough in his attention to the details of supervising the changing situation. He must follow closely the progress of the change. He must ensure that he receives a constant flow of accurate and timely information about what is happening 'on the shop floor'. He must maintain close contact with his subordinate supervisors and ensure that all of the myriad and seemingly trivial difficulties that inevitably accompany any change get solved before they burgeon into major problems. Finally, he must ensure that the necessary supporting activities (e.g. training, systems of wage and salary determination, engineering, quality control, economic evaluation, etc.) are provided in a useful form.

Still further, the manager must himself be personally flexible and adaptable to change. He must be able to view the developing situation objectively. He must be able to maintain the focus of his attention on the objectives of the change and not on any single method of their accomplishment. Furthermore, he should not be preoccupied with any possible implications of his approach for his personal status and career. The accomplishment of the task and the achievement of the goal should be his principal personal objectives. He should understand that the succesful accomplishment of such objectives is a particularly effective means for furthering his personal advancement and improving his status within the organization.

When a manager understands this concept, he is often better able to maintain a dispassionate and objective view of the changing scene. Thus, he can remain uncommitted to any single approach to the change, and can be better able to modify or alter his approach when this seems to be justified by the developing circumstances.

Finally, the manager should have a clear concept of his role in instituting and implementing a change. Earlier, we noted that the interdependence of the manager and his subordinates (and staff specialists) is particularly acute during periods of change. For this reason, the more conventional and authoritarian methods of managing such as delegating and following up, checking, and applying pressure when performance fails to meet expectations, are likely to be less productive than a more indirect approach. Thus, the manager should regard his role less in terms of a 'director of operations' and more in terms of a 'facilitator of communications and developer of understanding' between people with different points of view.

> I do not mean that the executive should spend his time with the different people concerned discussing the human problems of change as such. He *should* discuss schedules, technical details, work assignments, and so forth. But he should also be watching closely for the messages that are passing back and forth as people discuss these topics. He will find that people—himself as well as others—are always implicitly asking and making answers to questions like: 'How will he accept criticism?' 'How much can I afford to tell him?' 'Does he really get my point?' 'Is he playing games?' The answers to such questions determine the degree of candour and the amount of understanding between the people involved.
>
> When the administrator concerns himself with these problems and acts to facilitate understanding, there will be less log-rolling and more sense of common purpose, fewer words and better understanding, less anxiety and more acceptance of criticism, less griping and more attention to specific prob-

lems—in short, better performance in putting new ideas for technological change into effect.[1]

Thus, when a manager decides that his immediate objective is to develop understanding, and when he shapes his actions so as to catalyse such development instead of behaving like a more traditional manager, he is improving his chances for achieving the change successfully.

The 'ideal' manager (or supervisor) for a situation where a change must be introduced and implemented should possess the following qualities:

Intelligence
Imagination
A mind that is analytical and logical
Sensitivity to and consideration for the needs of others
Ability to be a good listener
Skill in communications, particularly oral
Skill in persuasion
Personal objectivity and detachment with respect to the change
Personal flexibility and adaptability in his approach to the change
Understanding of his special role requirements during periods of change

The closer a manager comes to having these characteristics, the greater will be the probability that any changes for which he is responsible will be successfully realized.

Development of Managerial Abilities

By the time one becomes adult, many of the above qualities have become well developed and established elements of one's personality. It would be difficult to bring about any substantial changes in such deeply rooted characteristics as intelligence, imagination, fundamental attitudes towards the self and towards other people, and the ability to be analytical, logical, systematic and thorough. Even the development of the skills of listening, communication and persuasion depend to a considerable extent on certain fundamental aspects of personality. It is improbable that any manager

[1] P. R. Lawrence, 'How to deal with resistance to change', *The Harvard Business Review*, **32**, No. 3, May–June 1954.

with modest abilities and fixed attitudes could ever develop his capabilities to the extent required for truly effective management of changes.

But, on the other hand, there is no assurance that a manager with the requisite potential will necessarily be able to develop and apply his abilities effectively. The organizational climate or environment can be an important factor in controlling this development and application. These abilities can be either stimulated or inhibited by the structure and the cultural beliefs and norms of the organizational environment.

One of these organizational characteristics is the extent to which change is a continuing, normal, regular everyday activity in the organization as a whole. It is especially difficult to accomplish changes in an organization addicted to the *status quo,* and where any change is a rare event. In such a climate, managers would find it difficult to gain any experience with the problems of introducing and implementing changes. Furthermore, when changes are instituted, the shock effect would probably result in intense resistance, not only from the workers, but also from the lower levels of supervision and staff specialists. On the other hand, in an organization where changes are a frequent and normal occurrence, it would be difficult for the *status quo* to become entrenched. People's expectations would be more geared to change. Hence, their resistance would tend to be less strong than in the first case. Also, managers and supervisors would have ample opportunity to become skilled in bringing about changes and in coping with all of the attendant problems.

Another significant aspect of the organizational climate is the extent to which the responsibility for managing changes is considered a normal, regular part of the jobs of all line managers and supervisors. In some organizations, the middle and lower levels of line management do not regard it as their responsibility to introduce and implement changes. Instead, they believe this to be the responsibility of senior management and staff specialists (e.g. industrial engineers, organization and methods specialists, employee relations, etc.). These middle- and lower-level managers and supervisors regard their jobs as being concerned primarily with administering and coordinating a set of existing and established conditions. They would consider it somebody else's job to change these conditions.

Where such a view persists, it would be difficult to gain the involvement and commitment of these lower-level supervisors to the realization of changes. These managers and supervisors would probably not identify with the objectives of senior management. When confronted with any resistance to a change by their subordinates, these managers and supervisors would be unlikely to find ways to lessen such resistance. In fact, they would tend to resist the change themselves. In such an organizational climate, the senior managers would have to assume the role of prime mover in accomplishing any change. This circumscribed concept of the managerial job can only inhibit the development and application of the requisite abilities and skills for managing changes.

How do lower-level supervisors develop an attitude that the responsibility for making changes and improving conditions is not theirs but rather somebody else's? Probably the most important reason is that senior management have failed to make this responsibility an explicit part of the supervisor's job. For example, in evaluating and discussing supervisory performance, competence in the achievement of changes would normally not be one of the criteria considered or used as a basis for rewards.

Without such a stimulus, it is unlikely that most supervisors would be willing to risk taking any initiative in managing changes. The chances for failure simply are too great. Accomplishing any change is far more difficult than maintaining operations on a smoothly functioning 'even keel'. When changes are initiated, there is much risk of 'rocking the boat' by generating resentment, anxiety and insecurity. Also, when a manager or supervisor undertakes to bring about a change, the fact of his interdependence with his subordinates is particularly highlighted. Because of this interdependence, most changes are difficult to accomplish through the traditional managerial methods that depend on the use of authority and control. Many a manager or supervisor would feel considerable discomfort in a situation where he could not rely on his accustomed ways of managing. Thus, unless senior management deliberately establish the responsibility for managing changes as part of the jobs of lower-level managers and supervisors, these subordinate members of management would be unlikely to accept such responsibility on their own initiative.

Some independence of middle mangement from arbitrary pressures imposed by senior management is another necessary characteristic of the organizational climate, if there is to be stimulation of the development and application of those supervisory abilities needed to make changes. The timing of management's actions in a changing situation is often a key variable in determining the outcome. The manager with the direct responsibility for results should have the greatest possible latitude for making decisions and taking action relevant to the change. He should be able to time and relate his actions to the requirements of the developing situation. These changing events should be the primary factors that he considers before deciding what to do next. Any arbitrary external pressure directed at him from higher levels in the organization may circumscribe his freedom to act in accordance with these events.

We must, however, distinguish between arbitrary, unjustified intervention and those senior management directives based on sound, considered judgements. This latter kind of decision should shape the entire strategy for accomplishing the change. On the other hand, when arbitrary deadlines or any other unjustified demands are imposed on a manager by his seniors, the introduction of these factors may reduce his ability to achieve the maximum benefits from the change.

Such arbitrary and unjustified interventions are commonplace. For example, during the process of a change, senior management might issue a request, 'suggestion' or even an order which may be inconsistent with the plan as it was established initially. Or, senior management's expectations of the change may be unrealistic. Certainly, poor and irrational decisions are made in every organization.

However, it is essential that the effects of such irrational decisions be minimized. This is possible when the manager directly responsible for the change can tell his senior managers directly and truthfully what are likely to be the consequences of their directives on the success of that change. The organizational climate should be such that his judgement and comments are given serious consideration before senior management insist that their orders be implemented.[1] Where such a climate exists, managers and supervisors are encouraged to develop and apply those qualities necessary for realizing changes successfully.

There is yet another necessary characteristic of the organizational climate for managers and supervisors to be effective in their handling of changes. Most members of management should be so orientated that they tend to place greatest value on the accomplishment of a task or goal. Thus, when a manager faces a problem requiring his decision and action, he should first ask himself, 'What course of action should be taken that would probably result in the

[1] This might be considered in the same light as the 'upward influence' discussed on pp. 26–27.

most effective solution to the problem? What action would be likely to produce the best long-term results for the company as a whole?' His first consideration should *not* be, 'What action should I take that would be most likely to further my own status and career within the company? How can I ensure that if all goes well I shall get the credit, and if problems arise, I shall not be held responsible?'

Several benefits could result from an organizational value system that ranks successful task accomplishment uppermost, and that places personal and political considerations lower down the value scale. One such benefit is that the task-orientated manager should be more open to criticism of his methods for approaching the change when such criticism is valid and is directed towards improving the possibilities for success. He should also be more likely to accept others' ideas and suggestions. Thus, such a manager would be more likely to encourage the involvement and participation of others in formulating some of the decisions affecting the conduct and outcome of the change. Also, such a manager would be more likely to share information about the change fully and honestly with all concerned. He would not be tempted to enhance his own power by withholding information, and would realize that he could often lessen resistance to the change by communicating more fully about it.

Additionally, the manager who values task accomplishment above personal status would probably have a greater willingness to experiment with fresh ideas and to risk failure. Carefully controlled experiments that fail can often yield valuable insights about methods of solving problems. This fact is fully recognized by scientists and engineers. In the culture of the laboratory or development group, the failure of an experiment is not regarded as a personal failure. Yet in the culture of management, such is often not the case.

For many managements, any kind of a failure, whether it be experimental or not, is most typically equated with personal failure. Consequently, managers are not willing to expose themselves to the risks inherent in experimentation. They are reluctant to try out any ideas or suggestions that depart from well-trodden paths because such ventures often are vulnerable to failure. If, on the other hand, the consequences of experimental failure in a changing situation are perceived as constructive and leading ultimately to enhanced possibilities for success, a manager would probably be more willing to try out approaches departing from the norm. Such constructive perceptions of experimentation and failure are possible when managers at all levels are concerned primarily with accomplishing the task.

How can one develop such a constructive attitude towards sharing information, accepting criticism and ideas from other people, and towards experimentation and failure? How can the value system of an organization be restructured so that task accomplishment is ranked above personal and political considerations? Perhaps the most important factor influencing the development of any value system in an organization is the basis on which its members are rewarded. There must be an evident relationship between task accomplishment and personal reward in terms of both economic and non-economic rewards (e.g. advancement, status). Then, task accomplishment will assume primary importance in management's value structure. On the other hand, task accomplishment will often be regarded as secondary if the people promoted or otherwise rewarded seem to be talented primarily in political astuteness and the ability to turn every situation to their own personal advantage. In such an organization, when he is about to make a decision, almost any manager's first concern will be for the consequences of his act relative to his personal future with the company. Thus, by carefully controlling the criteria on which rewards are based, senior management can influence strongly the nature of the established value system in their organization.

Finally, senior management control another organizational characteristic which can influence the development and application of those managerial qualities desirable for making changes. This is the extent to which senior management understand and recognize that lower-level managers and supervisors can resist changes in the same way and for similar reasons as do any other group of employees.

The senior management that truly understand this point would tend to encourage their lower-level managers and supervisors to participate as fully as possible in making the decisions relevant to any change. These senior managers would take care to ensure that the individual fears, hopes and other personal needs of the other members of supervision will receive as much attention as will the fears, hopes and other personal needs of the workers. An uneasy and resentful manager or supervisor cannot be expected to cope effectively with the fears of an apprehensive worker. A deliberate policy of involving the lower levels of management in formulating those decisions relevant to accomplishing a change, will ensure that all members of management are united in a 'common front' when they introduce and implement that change. Such a unified approach is possible only when senior management have deliberately developed a team attitude and approach encompassing all levels of management.

Another view of the characteristics necessary in an organization where changes can be introduced and implemented smoothly is proposed by R. Likert.[1] He suggests that the central problem is 'not how to reduce or eliminate potential conflict, but how to deal constructively with conflict'. He hypothesizes that an organization must have three characteristics for this to be possible.

> 'The organization must possess the machinery to deal constructively with conflict. This includes an organizational structure which facilitates constructive interaction between persons and between work groups. Furthermore, the organization's personnel must be skilled in the processes of effective interaction and mutual influence. These skills include those of leadership and membership roles, and of group building and maintenance functions. Finally, there must be a high level of confidence and trust among the members of the organization in each other, a high degree of loyalty to the work group, and a high degree of loyalty to the organization. Such confidence, trust and loyalty leads to earnest, sincere and determined efforts to find solutions to conflicts. These solutions can be highly creative and can represent better solutions than any stemming initially from the conflicting interests.
>
> 'An organization, therefore, must have an interaction and mutual influence process such that, consistent with their goals and needs, all persons who have an interest in the organization and its activities are able to exert at least some influence on the overall objectives and decisions of the organization, as well as to be influenced by them.
>
> 'In every organization, it is important to have an interaction and mutual influence mechanism which achieves and maintains the highest possible level of compatibility between the goals of the individuals who are in the organization or affected by it, and the overall objectives of the organization. . . . A maximum degree of compatibility should exist, but only

[1] R. Likert, in *Modern Organization Theory* (ed. M. Haire), Wiley, New York, 1959, p. 204.

between those goals and objectives which are important for the continued operation and effective functioning of the organization.

'In every healthy organization, there is, consequently, a continuous process of examining and modifying individual goals and organizational objectives, as well as the methods and rewards for achieving them. This continuous process is necessary for the objectives, methods and rewards to fit new developments and changing circumstances.

'In an organization in which there exists widespread acceptance of the objectives coupled with pride in these objectives, and in which the objectives and goals of the sub-units are consistent with the overall objectives of the organization, the efforts of the members will be highly focused and polarized. This polarization will mean that the behaviour of all members will be in the direction best suited to help the organization achieve its objectives.'

Summary

The following characteristics are typical of an organizational climate where managers and supervisors are encouraged to develop and apply those qualities necessary for the effective management of changes:

* *Change is considered as a continuing, normal, everyday activity for everyone in the organization. Changes are a frequent occurrence.*

* *Introducing and implementing changes are considered the responsibility of line managers and supervisors.*

* *The manager responsible for making the change is delegated as much as possible of the responsibility and freedom of action to achieve the change. The influence of any arbitrary and unjustified pressures or interventions by senior management can be minimized if the manager's objections are considered seriously by his seniors.*

* *When making decisions, most managers and supervisors consider task accomplishment as a more important immediate personal objective than they do the direct pursuit of political and personal aims.*

* *Senior management understand and recognize the attitudes and needs of the lower-level managers and supervisors with respect to the change and its consequences.*

The last three of the above characteristics can occur in an organization only when there is mutual respect, trust and confidence between senior and middle management, and between middle management and the first-line supervisors. If the objectives of the organization are to be achieved successfully, such a mutuality of trust must be based on a recognition of the fact that all levels of management are interdependent on one another. Similiarly, it must be recognized that there is an interdependence between all of managment and the workers.

In any situation of mutual trust, there is inherent a risk that problems may be handled by the lower levels of management in quite a different manner from the way in which senior managers might have handled them. However, for that trust to exist, it must be accompanied by a measure of confidence that, although such problems may not be solved in precisely the expected way, the desired results will nevertheless be achieved. If, through experience, senior management find their trust to be unjustified, then they should re-evaluate the competence of that individual to whom they delegated the responsibility. It is not the concept of mutual trust that should be reconsidered.

True delegation of the full responsibility and the freedom to act when making a change must be accompanied by mutual feelings of respect, trust and confidence. Only in such a climate can the managers and supervisors be more concerned with task accomplishment than they are with the furtherance of their personal aims. Only in such a climate can senior management develop a vertically integrated managerial and supervisory group that functions like a team. And only in such a climate are management likely to achieve a high proportion of successes in their realization of changes.

Conclusion

Introducing and implementing a change so that the anticipated benefits are fully realized is one of the most complicated and difficult aspects of the manager's job. To solve the problems and to minimize resistance requires that a manager apply fully his intellect, imagination and skills of perception and communication. Coping successfully with a change is also a test of the manager's sensitivity to and concern for the needs and goals of other people. In short, the effective realization of a change is a stringent test of any manager's total abilities. And the success with which the anticipated benefits are achieved is dependent, in large measure, on the extent of that manager's abilities.

Thus, those periods when changes are being carried out in an organization can be the times when the most effective development of managerial talent and abilities is taking place. Thus, the process of introducing and implementing changes can be regarded as a crucible for management development. Genuine development will occur only when managers and supervisors are helped by their immediate superiors to learn the most fruitful lessons from both their successes and their failures. Without such guidance and coaching, the full benefit might not be realized from these experiences. Also, some wrong lessons might be learned as well.

Although accomplishing changes presents formidable problems that are difficult of solution, the probabilities for success can nevertheless be increased significantly. Certainly, although there is no neat formula to guarantee this in every case, senior management can improve their chances for success by taking the following steps:

* *Establish and maintain an organizational climate that stimulates the development and application of those managerial qualities necessary for the effective achievement of changes. The essential characteristics of such a climate are described above.*

* *When a change must be accomplished, delegate the responsibility and the freedom to act to a manager whose qualities and abilities most closely resemble those previously described.*

* *Ensure that the change is planned, discussed, introduced and followed up systematically, applying the concepts outlined in this book.*

* *Ensure that the manager receives support and assistance in whatever action is justified, to minimize any resistance to the change, and to increase the possibilities for its acceptance.*

Thus, when a management team is unified in its understanding and attitudes, and when they approach any change objectively and systematically, they should be able to achieve, in most cases, their expected benefits.

Index